Outwitting Housework

Outwitting Housework

Brilliant Tips, Tricks, and Advice on Housekeeping . . . and Life

Nancy Rosenberg

Illustrations by Laurie Heidorn

THE LYONS PRESS
Guilford, Connecticut
An imprint of The Globe Pequot Press

The Lyons Press is an imprint of The Globe Pequot Press.

10 9 8 7 6 5 4 3 2 1

Printed in the United Stated of America

Designed by Stephanie Doyle

ISBN 1-59228-349-7

Library of Congress Cataloging-in-Publication Data is available on file.

Contents

Introduction

You probably picked up this book because you want your house to be cleaner and more organized, but you're not willing to spend the rest of your life with a dust rag in hand. You're tired of clutter, of being embarrassed by the condition of your home if friends drop by unexpectedly. You want to gain a measure of control over your surroundings, but don't know where to start.

For many of us, the very idea of housework is daunting. Few things in life have the ability to sap our energy like the pressure of establishing and then maintaining a clean, orderly home. To a certain degree this phenomenon is due to the fact that, by definition, housework is never-ending. No sooner have you mopped the floor than a person or a pet walks back into the room; even as your dust rag grazes the tops of furniture, more dust is hovering in the air nearby, waiting for you to turn your back, so it can settle peaceably, undisturbed.

You have a few options. You can spend your retirement fund on housekeepers and cleaning services. You can give up and resign yourself to living in less-than-ideal surroundings. You can go to the other extreme and decide to whip your house into shape...even if it kills you. Or, you can approach the problem methodically, thoughtfully, and figure out a way to improve your surroundings without becoming a wild-eyed, vacuuming-under-the-feet-of-guests, obsessive-compulsive cleaning lunatic.

In other words, the idea is not to spend all your time cleaning. The idea is to clean efficiently, to clean well, and to only clean the things that need it. We all know or have heard about people who are so obsessed with cleaning that that is just about the only thing they do, and the fact is that maintaining a home *does* require a lot of work. It can consume your life if you let it. *Outwitting Housework* means being in control of your house, as opposed to letting your house control you.

What you will find in *Outwitting Housework* are hundreds of ideas to make the process easier. I hate housework, but I love having a clean house. I refuse to spend one unnecessary minute of my life scouring, scrubbing, or rinsing. This book is about shortcuts, about simple, easy ways to reclaim your castle from the forces of filth. Think *easy*, *effective*, and occasionally *unorthodox*. Whatever it is you have, there's probably an easy way to clean it, and this book will tell you how.

As we prepare to work together to make your house the clean, comfortable home you desire, keep in mind that change of any kind is seldom comfortable. We want things to be different, but we don't want to do anything differently than we've done it in the past! Change can be unwieldy and uncomfortable, like trying on a new pair of shoes. It's all too easy to give up the stiff, shiny new shoes and hang on to the well-worn, comfortable ones, but when we do that, metaphorically speaking, we give up something better to hang on to something that is old and tattered.

When we hang on to old patterns of behavior, whether it's a job we hate, a relationship that just isn't working, or an ineffective style of home maintenance, we forfeit what could have been if only we had been brave enough to let go of the familiar and embrace the promise of the unknown. Remember: *A ship has to lose sight of land before it can discover new worlds.* Allow yourself the freedom to give up some old habits. The promise of the new is a clean, well-run house you'll be proud to call home.

Chapter One

Gloves

Paper

Towels

Toilet
Brush

Blea[ch]

mop

Bowl Cleaner

Broom

Glass

Bucket

Rags

Cleaner

L. Kilborn

JUST THE BASICS:
A HOUSEKEEPING PRIMER

Maintaining an orderly home with a minimum of effort is a lofty goal. "Impossible," you may be tempted to mutter. But it's not impossible. There are five basic principles that, once internalized, can make this a reality even for those who are seriously challenged in the clean-house department. You will notice as you read this book that the basic ideas behind many of the strategies hearken back to these five basic truths.

5 Basic Principles for Outwitting Housework

PRINCIPLE #1: UNDERSTAND THE VALUE OF ADEQUATE STORAGE

Determine how much storage space you have. If you live in a chic but cramped 600-square-foot urban apartment, you have to come to terms with the fact that you simply don't have room for an extensive wardrobe, thousands of tapes and CDs, a menagerie of pets, or a world-class collection of plates, beer steins, or porcelain figurines. If space is limited—and for most of us it is—you'll have to learn to be ruthless in determining what you truly need and what items you can (happily) live without. If you don't have adequate storage space for your possessions, you are doomed to forever live in a cluttered space.

PRINCIPLE #2: HAVE A PLACE FOR EVERYTHING

Once you have determined how much storage space you have, the next step is to figure out how that space can best be used. Utilizing space efficiently and even creatively can make the difference between a cluttered or an organized home. Determining what goes where, then putting things where they belong, is key.

PRINCIPLE #3: LOOK FOR SHORTCUTS

When it comes to housecleaning, perfectionists insist that everything be done "the right way." As if the Purist Police are going to come knockin' if you vacuum "just the middles" or dust around a few doohickeys. Look for ways to take shortcuts. If you can scrub the ring from around the tub while you're still in the bath, more power to you; you'll save not only your knees but also the need to do the chore later. Look for ways to clean *smarter*, not *more*.

PRINCIPLE #4: MAKE PEACE WITH IMPERFECTION

In his book *Don't Sweat the Small Stuff...and It's All Small Stuff*, author Richard Carlson, Ph.D., says something profound. He says, "I have yet to meet an absolute perfectionist whose life is filled with inner peace." Put another way by another sage: "The *best* is the enemy of the *good*" (Voltaire). An entire subset of frustrated homemakers exists because they are perfectionists who can't find the time or energy to "do things right," so they don't do them *at all*. For perfectionists, it is comforting to realize that the entire house doesn't have to be spotless. Do a little bit here and there, do what you can, have others pitch in to help, and, although the end result may not be perfect, it will certainly be an improvement.

Decide how clean is clean enough, then be willing to let the rest of it go. So what if you haven't wiped out the kitchen cabinets in a year? Who cares if there are dust bunnies under the beds? Do you really want to spend your limited free time cleaning in the backs of cupboards or beneath beds? This isn't to say that you never tackle these jobs, but the point is that you decide when, where, and how much cleaning you need to do.

PRINCIPLE #5: UNDERSTAND THE VALUE OF A SIMPLE LIFE

Philosopher and sage Lao-tzu said this: "Manifest plainness, embrace simplicity, reduce selfishness, have few desires." In more recent times much has been made of the value of living a simpler life. What does this mean? To borrow a few stock phrases, it means *quality over quantity*, it means *less is more*. Paring down a lavish, complicated lifestyle leaves more room for the people and pastimes in your life that really matter. Living a simple life means different things to different people. You may need to cut back on your social commitments, declutter a few rooms, cut up a few credit cards, drive a more modest car or live in a smaller home. You may need to actively sustain five quality friendships, as opposed to juggling a crowd of fifty. You may need to have your kids make some difficult choices: they may need to pick one or two sports or hobbies instead of having three or four. Or maybe you need to look for a job that is better suited to your talents and disposition.

The Housekeeper's Prayer

Lord, thank you for this mess before me,
because it means that I am blessed with abundance.

When I am surrounded by mountains of laundry,
remind me that there are those who have no clothes.
When I despair at the piles of dirty dishes,
help me remember that there are those who have no food.
When toys clutter every room,
help me to remember that there are those who have no children.
When I am overwhelmed by housework,
help me to remember that there are those who have
no floor to sweep, no bed to make, no bathtub to clean.

Keep me mindful of my blessings, Lord,
and help me to recognize the
signs of abundance.

Where to Begin? Getting in the Right Frame of Mind

Don't think of housekeeping as cleaning, or chores, or drudgery. Don't think of it in negative terms. Instead, see this as a gift you give to yourself. See this as a tool that will make your life easier, less complicated, and more manageable.

There is an art to running a household well. You can sloppily fold a basket of clothes, or you can carefully match corners and hems, and the resulting basket of freshly laundered garments speaks volumes. What does it say? It says that someone cares, that someone is paying attention to the details. Just a little more effort in some things can make a great deal of difference.

Baking or Barbecuing?

I have a friend whose mother is a compulsive cleaner. This woman will miss family reunions held down the street because her spice rack needs to be cleaned and organized. Clearly, she has a problem, but her compulsive cleaning has rubbed off a bit on my friend. Because her mother cleans so meticulously, my friend feels that cleaning nooks and crannies with a toothbrush and scrubbing floors on her hands and knees is the "right" way to clean.

There is an analogy we can use here that is apt: cleaning is not baking, it is barbecuing. When you bake, every ingredient has to be carefully measured. You have to follow the recipe carefully. If you omit a step or substitute an ingredient, the recipe will not turn out well.

Then there is barbecuing. You throw a bunch of marinade ingredients in a bowl, toss the vegetables or meat, let it sit a while, then pop it on the grill. Ingredients don't need to be measured; it's just "a little bit of this," and "a little bit of that."

There is no one "right" way to clean anything. It's like barbecuing. You can figure out how you like things and go from there. There are lots of different ways to clean just about anything.

You can dust with lemon oil, with mineral oil and a squeeze of lemon, with a rag dampened with water, or with a premoistened towelette.

You can move furniture to vacuum and move the appliance in careful, symmetric lines until the entire carpet has been covered, or you can vacuum "just the middles."

You can wash the dishes by hand or use the dishwasher. You can dry them with a towel or let them air-dry. Or you can use a hair dryer. Or put the dishes outside to dry in the sun. The point is that there is no one "right" way. Give up your notions of how things "should be done." This is your house. You get to clean it the way you want to.

Now, that said, some cleaning methods are easier and more efficient than others. I'd use a towel to dry hand-washed dishes before I'd use the hair dryer, for example. This book is about helping you find the easiest way, about finding the way that works best *for you*.

Make Time for Yourself

Stephen Covey talks about the importance of *sharpening the saw*, of keeping your mental tools sharp and efficient and in good working order so that the work you do will go smoothly.

For the homemaker this translates into the importance of staying mentally sharp and rejuvenated. If you attack a pile of clutter when you are exhausted, stressed, and cranky, for example, then you will be in no frame of mind to efficiently wade through the pile. The job will be much harder than it needs to be.

Work on that same pile of clutter when you are fresh and well rested, and the job will be much easier. You will be better able to decide what to keep, what to toss, and where to file the important letters or documents that you run across.

The key is in making time for yourself so that you can approach housekeeping with a fresh, well-rested mindset. If you let yourself get run into the ground, then your mental and physical well-being will suffer—along with the general state of your house.

Take the time you need—*on a regular basis*—to keep your mental saw sharp.

"*Yeah, right.*" I can hear you snickering. "*Where am I going to find extra time for myself?*"

If you really want to find the time, you can, though you may have to carefully analyze your current habits and pastimes in order to determine where you can regain lost or inefficiently used minutes and hours.

KICK THE LATE-NIGHT HABIT

"Early to bed, early to rise, makes a man healthy, wealthy and wise." It's a ditty we've heard since childhood, wise words from Benjamin Franklin. He also said this: "He that riseth late must trot all day." A Spanish proverb puts it this way: "God helps those who get up early."

Turn it around. Here's a great way to lose valuable time and begin each day in a frenzy: Hit the snooze button as many times as you possibly can. Once your feet finally hit the floor, you realize that you're already late getting ready for work or waking up the kids for school. You holler at the kids to WAKE UP!!—thereby ensuring that their day gets off to a frantic beginning. No time for breakfast—a cold Pop Tart will have to do. You rush out the door and find—what's this? A traffic jam? Now you're *really* late. Bad words come to mind. Oops—a few of them slipped out.

This is really not a good way to start the day, yet this very scene plays out in homes up and down your street every day—but it doesn't have to be this way.

In many cases the problem starts not in the morning but the night before. It *is* hard to wake up when you haven't had enough sleep. Staying up late is a luxury that few of us can afford.

"But I'm a night owl. I could never go to bed before 12, much less 10. I get so much done at night. That's the only time I have for myself."

A compromise solution may be in order, for the harsh reality is that night owls tend to fritter away those late-night/early-morning hours, puttering around, watching TV, reading, surfing the Net, but the price they pay for these luxurious hours of solitude is often steep.

For some reason, hours reclaimed in the early morning tend to be more productive. The day is new, the sun is warm and welcoming, and the things you are able to accomplish subtract more easily from your

"To Do" list. The paper gets read. You have the time to prepare and then enjoy a nutritious breakfast. If you have kids, you have time to tend to their needs, too. They aren't rushed. School papers get signed. Important notes to teachers get written. For some reason these things don't usually get accomplished in the wee hours. The early-morning hours better facilitate the important things, or what really needs to get done.

How to go about taking advantage of these early-morning hours?

You may need to start slow. Start by going to bed just 20 or 30 minutes earlier than you usually do. Set the stage to sleep well. Avoid caffeine late in the day. Many people find that a warm shower before bed helps them sleep better. A warm bath is another way to help induce sound, satisfying sleep. Turn off the television. Watching a fast-paced action thriller before bed (or the 11 o'clock news, for that matter) is not a great way to induce sleep.

Reading before bed is an effective, time-honored way to help your mind and body slow down and prepare for slumber. Don't read anything related to work, and try to avoid reading material that causes you to worry or fret about unresolved issues in your life, such as how to deal with a wayward teenager or resolve financial difficulties. The idea is to allow your body and mind to slowly power down. Read until the words begin to blur on the page, until your reading becomes so slow that you're practically asleep already.

Once your bedtime routine has been modified effectively, move it up a notch. Instead of going to bed at 11:30, try 11. While some need more sleep than others, a good rule of thumb is to allow yourself eight good hours of uninterrupted sleep. If you need to be up no later than 6:30, then a good goal would be to get up at 6, to carve some unhurried time out for yourself, which means you need to aim for going to sleep at 10.

I know that this can be a tall order for night owls, but if you find that you crave additional time for yourself, and if your mornings are hurried and chaotic, then you just might want to give this new approach a try. Outwitting housework will be much easier when you are well-rested and refreshed. Don't take my word for it—listen to Ben Franklin!

4 Ways to Add Hours to Your Day

There are other times in the day that are ripe for reclaiming lost minutes and hours. Eliminating time spent watching television is a no-brainer. Here are some other ways to make use of time you may be using inefficiently:

- ✦ **Learn to identify wasted time.** What do you do while you wait for popcorn to pop in the microwave, for example? Here you have three or four minutes—time to rinse and load a stack of dishes, feed the cat, water the houseplants, or take a damp paper towel and quickly clean a few mystery globs off the floor.

- ✦ **Take care of household chores when it makes sense to do so.** For example, clean the shower when you're in it. You're already wet.

- ✦ **Make household tasks *easy* to do.** Keep stashes of cleaning products in the rooms where they will be used. Having a container of disinfecting towelettes beneath every sink makes it easy to grab one and give the sink a quick wipe, for example. Cleaning doesn't have to be a big production.

- ✦ **Figure out where your time needs to be better spent.** I have a tendency, for example, to spend too much time reading the newspaper in the mornings. At the same time, I have a desk in my kitchen that tends to collect stacks of paper clutter. When I take a step back and look at my morning routine objectively, I can see that my life would run more smoothly if I cut 10 minutes from my morning paper routine and spent that time instead working on my desktop clutter. Without this bit of objective reasoning it is easy for me to while away the hours with my morning coffee and paper, but with a small amount of analysis I can easily see that I would rather pare down my luxurious paper time and have a clean desk to show for it. I can do both—I just have to make a conscious effort to add some structure to this time of day.

The 80/20 Rule

A general rule of business states that 80 percent of the work is done by 20 percent of the workforce. This same principle holds true in many other areas of life, including time management. Many of us accomplish 80 percent of the work we need to do around the house in only 20 percent of our available time to do it. What happens to the rest of the time? It is used inefficiently, lost to the repercussions of poor planning and inadequate time management.

Translation, please?

Get into the habit of using time consciously, as opposed to allowing it to slip away. This simple shift in perception has the dramatic ability to literally add hours of productive time to your day. Many of us have wasted time built into our schedules that we can reclaim with only a bit of determination. The biggest time wasters tend to be watching television, surfing the Net, and engaging in leisurely telephone chats.

While I am not suggesting that you sell your television, disconnect your Internet service, and quit talking to your mom or your friends on the phone, it could be that these seemingly innocuous pastimes have been robbing you of the clean, orderly house you desire.

For example, if you analyze your daily schedule, you may realize that, on average, you spend two hours watching television. Maybe more. Let's say you watch two shows every day. Now, if you were to decide which of those two shows you most enjoy, you could still spend a leisurely hour watching television, but by turning off the tube after just one show you would reclaim an hour of valuable time *every day*. Seven hours a week. That's enough time to have a sparkling clean house *all the time*.

Others find that cleaning while they watch TV or listen to a favorite radio program is a very effective way to kill the proverbial two birds with one stone. While you may not be able to clean the whole house, you may find that in a half hour or so you'll be able to dust the living room, clean the windows or blinds, or fold a load of laundry or two. The idea here is to actively look for time during your daily routine that can be reclaimed; in most cases, TV time fits the bill.

Realizing Your Value

Every so often a study comes out that breaks down the jobs most home-makers do, assigns an hourly rate to each job, then assumes that every homemaker does the jobs of all those professions eight hours a day, five days a week. The end result, or tally of annual potential earnings, soon approaches the $500,000 mark, which is probably a tad unrealistic.

However, the fact remains that most homemakers *do* wear the hats of several different professionals. This is true whether or not you work outside the home; just because you have another job doesn't mean that household chores go away. We do the work of many. We multitask. Paying professionals to do what we do on a daily basis would quickly add up.

For example, the cost of a full-time housekeeper is approximately $15,000/year.

A full-time nanny? $18,000. An around-the-clock nanny? $35,000.

A part-time chauffeur or driving service? $3,000.

A personal chef and dietitian? $40,000.

A personal shopper? $8,000.

Using these estimates, the work done by an average homemaker is worth approximately $100,000/year. Now, let's deduct 25 percent, just because as a homemaker you have the option of letting a few things slide. You can order pizza or have fast food for dinner occasionally, for example, whereas a personal chef would promptly be fired for such culinary trespasses. So we end up with a ballpark figure of $75,000—quite a respectable sum.

When we see that the work we do as homemakers adds value—real value—then we can appreciate that the work we have before us is important. We don't mop the floor because we love mopping floors; we mop because it's important to live in a house that's clean, and having clean floors makes a difference. Living in unclean surroundings is demoralizing, even for children.

Once you see the intrinsic value in what you do as a homemaker and keeper of the house, you begin to assume a pride of ownership over your domain. You begin to see your surroundings as a reflection of your skills and capabilities. A well-run home is a testimony to the skills of the person in charge: you.

Getting Organized

The first rule of effective household organization: Make sure you are using your free time judiciously. Spend five minutes each morning making a plan for the day. This is not a "To Do" list, though you may include those items on your list, too. Instead, this is a chance to examine your real priorities. Think about who has a birthday coming up. Do you need to buy a gift for someone, or get a card in the mail? At the top of the list, write down the people you need to connect with that day. Do you need to spend some quality time with your friends, spouse, or kids? Write it down.

Once a week—Sunday evenings are good—take the time to sit down with your calendar and get a good feel for the week that lies ahead. Take note of the social events that are coming up. What nights will you be busy? What nights will you be free?

Use this organizational time to plan your weekly menus and draw up a shopping list. This may sound daunting, but it really doesn't take that long, and the end result is a solid, reliable road map for the week that lies ahead.

The next step is a true key not only to outwitting housework, but to truly gaining a sense of control over your house. As we've seen, in order to use your time efficiently, you need a plan, and the next step is to map out a plan—a strategy—for getting your household maintenance on a practical, workable schedule.

Get out your pen and paper and make a list. List each day of the week, and assign to that day one major household chore. Here's my list:

Monday	Clean floors
Tuesday	Dust
Wednesday	Change/launder sheets
Thursday	Doors/glass/windows
Friday	Bathrooms
Saturday	Kids' rooms/playroom
Sunday	Get organized/deal with clutter

This list is not arbitrary. I do the floors on Monday, for example, because the floors in my house tend to get really dirty over the weekend. If I know I'm going to clean them on Monday, then I don't get uptight about the mess over the weekend.

I clean the bathrooms on Friday because I like to go into the weekend with the whole house smelling fresh and clean.

I clean the kids' rooms and the playroom on Saturday, when the kids are home and can help. I use this time to teach them to do it themselves, and though they are too young to do it entirely by themselves, they are helping and they are learning and, gradually, they are getting better.

Now, do one load of laundry each day, and your basic household maintenance is done.

You may need to modify this plan to suit your family and your lifestyle, of course. One woman I know, the mother of four young kids, has to do a whopping *four* loads of laundry every day just to keep up—or so she says. Maybe she has a really tiny washing machine. At any rate, divide the amount of laundry you do in a week and break it down into small, manageable chunks. This is far less daunting than letting it pile into mountains for Laundry Day.

You may have noticed that the kitchen is conspicuously absent from my weekly list of chores. It is. This is because the kitchen is the most likely room in the house (my house, anyway) to get used, which means it is the most likely room in the house to get dirty, so I stay on top of it and clean the kitchen every day. While there are certain chores in the kitchen that aren't done on a daily basis (cleaning out the refrigerator, for example, or organizing the pantry), I do those jobs on an as-needed basis. They aren't done with enough frequency to make it onto the weekly list. Other parts of the kitchen are covered by the more general list, by the way. For example, when I do the floors on Monday, I do the kitchen floor as well.

So you've figured out how much time you can devote to keeping the house clean, you've portioned it out over the week, and you do a little each day. It may not look like you have a full-time maid, and the baseboards may get a little dusty, but you won't want to hide your head in shame if a neighbor drops by for a chat, and you can get about the business of living in a reasonably clean environment. You're home free.

Advice from the Pros

There are a few basic strategies for achieving and then maintaining order in your home. Here are a few tips from housecleaning professionals that can help:

- ✦ Avoid procrastination. Do a job as soon as you notice it needs to be done.

- ✦ Begin straightening a room by picking up large items, which provides immediate gratification, then working your way to smaller items.

- ✦ Do one room at a time. When you finish one room, move on to the next, but don't try to clean several rooms at once.

- ✦ Assemble a portable arsenal of cleaning products, and use the right product for the task at hand.

10 Cleaning Products You Need

There are lots of books on the market that can tell you how to clean everything from venetian blinds to wool rugs. While this is not a book about "how to clean," there are some basic tools you should have in your arsenal against filth. You can't keep your home clean without the right products and tools. Here are the basic things you need:

1. A heavy-duty all-purpose cleanser such as Pine-Sol or Mr. Clean
2. Windex or glass cleaner
3. A nonabrasive cleanser such as Soft Scrub or Bon Ami
4. An abrasive cleanser such as Ajax or Comet
5. Furniture polish such as lemon oil
6. Heavy-duty oven cleaner (most ovens are self-cleaning, but oven cleaner is still great for cleaning baked-on food remnants in pots and pans and on the cooktop)
7. Disinfecting wipes
8. Rubber gloves
9. An assortment of rags and old towels and T-shirts
10. A vacuum cleaner with attachments

Enlisting the Troops

If you live with others, then maintaining your home is not a battle you should fight alone. In fact, if you choose to go it alone, chances are good that the end results will be failure and frustration.

Cluttered homes don't just happen. It takes *people* to really foul things up. People leave their socks on the floor, toys in the hall, and coffee cups on the kitchen counter. I'm going to go out on a limb here and assume that you are not the only one in the house contributing to the mess. Odds are good that you have a partner, spouse, roommate, child, teen, or pet who is adding their fair share to the mess. Take comfort in the knowledge that you didn't make this mess by yourself, so you shouldn't have to clean it up by yourself, either.

Putting together a fair and balanced plan for maintaining a neat, clean abode is key. Divide chores up and let housemates or family members decide where they want to pitch in and help. It doesn't really matter what they want to do, as long as they do *something* and are pulling their own weight. Chores that no one wants should be divided equally; one person takes out the trash one day, then it's the next person's turn, for example.

You can add teeth to the system by agreeing beforehand on the consequences of not keeping up with the system. Maybe roommates can agree to pay a bit more of the rent if they fail to do their share and keep their part of the house or apartment clean. Kids can forfeit some of their allowance money if their chores are not done. (For more on motivating your kids to help around the house, see Chapter 9.)

Another way to enlist the troops is to schedule a time to clean, with everyone who lives under your roof pitching in to help clean at the same time. This can happen every day after dinner, for example, or once a week—or both, with the harder cleaning being done over the weekend. This type of arrangement has two benefits: the cleaning goes much faster when everyone is pitching in to help, and it's more fun to clean with someone else. Get out the cleaning supplies, put on some high-energy music, and the whole house or apartment will sparkle in no time.

"Many hands make light work."

—John Heywood
(c. 1497–c. 1580)

To Hire or Not to Hire Help

Before we get into the nitty-gritty of outwitting housework, let's examine a burning issue in detail: should you hire a housekeeper to help you keep your house in order?

This is not a rhetorical question. (I can hear your snorts of laughter.)

There are many of us who would love nothing more than an occasional, professional hand when it comes to housework, but this can be a difficult expense to justify.

Is there a solid, pragmatic way to determine whether or not you can afford to hire help? There is, and in fact this formula may very well indicate not only that you *can* afford to hire professional help, but that you *should*.

Here is how it works:

If you work, figure out how much you realistically earn per hour. It doesn't matter if you work inside or outside the home. Determine your hourly rate of compensation. If you can realistically expect to earn more per hour than it would cost you to hire help, then you should consider hiring someone to help you with housework. This is not to say that you need to have a housekeeper every day, or even every week. You can hire someone to come in just to help with "hard" cleaning every two weeks or even once a month: the furniture, floors, and bathrooms all get intensively cleaned by professionals, then you and your family do the maintenance work in between cleanings.

Others choose to hire professionals just for specific jobs, such as washing windows, steam-cleaning carpets, or yard work.

What if you don't make enough to justify the expense, or what if you don't work at all but your house is in a constant state of disarray, so you feel that you need help anyway?

There are several different approaches you can take, one of which you have already done just by picking up this book: you can figure out better, smarter, more efficient ways to tackle the clutter and messes in your home.

There may be extenuating circumstances that have contributed to the fact that your home is in a state of disarray. Maybe you're sick, have suffered an injury, are recovering from surgery, or just had a baby. Maybe you or someone you live with compulsively hangs on to things. Maybe you have eight children, four cats, and six dogs. Maybe you are caring for an elderly parent. Maybe you have a demanding job with a long workday and commute. There are times in life when keeping a tidy home is more difficult than at other times. Cut yourself a little bit of slack. If keeping up with housework is more than you are capable of, for whatever reason, then you may need to bite the bullet and hire someone to help you get control of things.

Another benefit to hiring someone to help with cleaning is often unanticipated: when a professional comes in to clean your home, you can observe this professional at work and learn lots of tricks of the trade. A professional cleaning person doesn't get sidetracked, they don't dawdle, they don't stop to read the mail or watch TV. They don't answer the phone or paint their toenails or file bills or water plants. They *clean*. They move efficiently and with purpose. They know what they're doing and have honed it into an art form. Odds are good that they won't want to stay in your house any longer than they have to: they are getting paid by the hour, and most housekeepers clean two or three or even four houses *every day*. If keeping your home neat and tidy and clean has become a challenge, hire it done, then pay close attention to the professionals as they work. You'll be amazed at the shortcuts you'll learn.

Before you pick up the phone to hire a housekeeper, however, consider the benefits you potentially forfeit when someone else assumes this work for you. Keeping a clean, orderly home yields many benefits, including a sense of instant gratification, a sense of accomplishment, and a potentially powerful sense of renewal. Feeling sluggish? An intensive bout of cleaning can restore energy levels, good vibes, and a positive attitude. Energetic cleaning can help banish anxiety, depression, and can help restore a sense of peace and contentment. In short, yes, cleaning is work, but, like many other types of difficult endeavors, there are definite, tangible rewards.

Make Your Home a Haven

Before you set about the task of cleaning, take a step back and consider the basic elements of your home. If you make your home a comfortable, relaxing, soothing place to be, then you will be more likely to want to keep it clean and straight. It's the whole pride-of-ownership thing. If your house is bleak and uncomfortable, then who cares if it's messy, but if it's your port in the storm then you'll want to take care of it. Here are some ideas for ways to cozy up your space and make it "yours."

FEATHER YOUR NEST

Futurist Faith Popcorn calls it "cocooning." My friend Lindsey says it's the best form of therapy she knows: When she needs to relax and take a break from the pressures of everyday life, she feathers her nest. Work on making your house a haven, a special place for you and your family and your treasures—your photos, mementos, the furniture and fabrics you have carefully selected. Surround yourself with things that make you happy.

The task of keeping your home clean and free of clutter is much easier if you are surrounded by an array of carefully chosen items. *Quantity* is not the idea here; *quality* is the goal. Free yourself of items that have no purpose or value. You want to be surrounded by things you love, things you *want* to keep clean and well-cared-for. Who wants to dust a boring, meaningless, cheap print in a plastic frame? But a priceless family portrait in a beautiful wood frame? You'll smile while you dust that one.

For me, an ideal room has a plant or two, including a big, leafy, silk ficus with white Christmas lights threaded through its branches. Books. Color. While some prefer subtle pastels or the crisp, clean look of white walls, I like bold swaths of color (we'll talk more about color in a minute). I like to display pictures of my family: black-and-white snapshots, not posed department store portraits. Cozy lamps, a flickering scented candle, my cat dozing in a corner somewhere or on my lap...there, in that room I am content. That's a room I want to keep clean. I don't mind keeping the floor vacuumed since this is a room I want to be in, and I want it to continue to look and feel nice.

As you set about making your house as warm, comfortable, and inviting as you possibly can, try to avoid utilitarian items that have no aesthetic appeal. For example, if you need a bookend, pass on the efficient gray metal model and opt instead for the bookend that will add to your décor. Even better, look for a bookend that you really like. This isn't rocket science, but making your house a haven is all about getting rid of extraneous items and surrounding yourself with things that have visual appeal.

Books, pictures, plants, and candles all can contribute to a warm, nurturing space, but be careful with accessories, and remember that fine line between *tasteful* and *too much*.

How do you know how much is too much?

Here's a good rule of thumb: If flat surfaces are difficult to dust, you may need to pare things down a bit. Give your eyes a place to rest. This rule applies to areas throughout your home. It doesn't matter if we're talking about a wall, a book shelf, or a desk top. Your eyes need a clean place to land, an occasional surface that is visually empty. If there aren't any empty spaces, you may have too much stuff.

SET THE MOOD WITH COLOR

Color is a fundamental element of every room that can help set the mood and tone in a dramatic way. Studies show that colors influence mood in a highly predictable manner: strong, bold colors tend to energize, while muted, soft tones tend to soothe and calm. This is why school classrooms and hospital rooms are generally painted with neutral colors such as beige or tan, while fast food restaurants are filled with neon oranges, reds, and yellows (*hurry up, eat, and leave!*)

Before you paint, determine the basic function of the room. Bold colors work well in the kitchen and dining room, while soothing, relaxing shades are natural picks for bedrooms. (*Never* paint a child's bedroom a bright color, unless you want an energizer bunny who refuses to sleep! Softer shades such as pale pink, blue, or lavender are better.)

After you've settled on a wall color, use a color wheel to help you determine complementary accent colors for contrasting trim, woodwork, flooring, curtains and furnishings. When using the wheel, the shade directly opposite any color is the ideal complement. You can determine the basic palette of a room by picking two or three adjacent colors, then using the color directly opposite the center or primary color to add a counterpoint of color for balance, harmony, and interest.

Shades of red and orange, used for wall or accent colors, ignite moods and spark both conversation and appetite. A dramatic red dining room can set the stage for lively dinner parties and sparkling conversation. A word here about lighting, however: Flat overhead lighting will make a red room seem garish. Use accent lighting, buffet lamps, wall sconces, candles, and a central light with a dimmer switch over the table to add drama and visual depth throughout the room. (For more on lighting, see below.)

Warm, earthy tones such as muted browns, corals, reds, and oranges draw you into a room with a cheery warmth and intimacy. Warm colors advance, making small rooms appear smaller and making large rooms seem more accessible. Wood tones, paneling, and even whole logs, like you find in log cabins, can make even a large space feel cozy and inviting.

Pale, cool colors tend to calm and soothe. Try a creamy seafoam green or sky blue to make a room feel cool and inviting. Cool colors tend to recede, making small spaces seem larger. They also make a room seem cooler, which makes them ideal choices for warm, sunny porches or sun-drenched rooms.

Pale blues, greens, and purples are meditative colors that encourage quiet, calm, and reflection. Stronger variations of these colors encourage creativity and contentment.

Consider light levels in a room when choosing colors, too. A bright, sunny room can handle darker shades, while an already dark room will seem like a cave if a dark shade is applied. However, a bright, sunny room may become unbearable if you add sunshine yellow paint. If you want a room to seem brighter, add a pale, clean color to perk things up visually.

If a room tends to accumulate clutter, consider using a lighter, paler shade of paint, which can lighten the mood and make the room seem less visually dense. Darker hues add visual weight to a room, which makes them perfect for law offices and home libraries, but these shades can be overpowering, so be careful before splashing saturated, heavy hues into an already crowded space. If a room feels cramped, consider painting the ceiling a lighter shade than the rest of the room. White works, but any shade significantly lighter than the color on the walls will work, too.

If you find yourself stuck over picking paint colors, you may find the preselected color palettes that paint stores offer to be of tremendous help in finalizing your color choices. Paint stores and home-improvement centers such as Lowe's and Home Depot have racks of color brochures, usually around the paint chips, that not only provide pictures of what rooms look like when they are painted a certain color, but they also provide complementary paint colors, so you can tell at a glance whether or not you like a certain color combination. These brochures amount to color cheat sheets: professional designers have done the legwork: all you have to do is pick a look you like and buy the paint.

While you're painting, consider your paint and color choice and factor in "the clean factor." Semigloss paints are much easier to clean than mattes, and darker, muted shades hide grime better than lighter colors. For walls that tend to attract a lot of smudges and fingerprints at lower levels you can install a chair rail and beadboard, which masks grime better than a flat wall. For areas higher up that tend to be repeatedly marred, such as around light switches, consider installing a larger switchplate, or even painting a decorative border around the switchplate in a semigloss or high-gloss paint, which easily wipes clean.

If you're in the mood to paint and have the slightest bent towards artistic expression, you may want to consider adding a bit of texture to your wall surface. Techniques such as rag-rolling or sponge painting can add a nice ambiance and are fun, inexpensive, and can do a great job masking dirt and grime. The look is more subtle than wallpaper, and an added bonus is that if you don't like the end result, you just paint right over it.

A final word in choosing paint: unless you're painting the attic, spend a bit more and buy high-quality paint. It goes on more smoothly, covers and holds up better, and is much easier to clean than the cheap stuff. Consider yourself warned.

If a room tends to accumulate clutter, consider using a lighter, paler shade of paint, which can lighten the mood and make the room seem less visually dense.

GET THE LIGHT RIGHT

Studies have shown that soft, natural, ambient lighting relaxes and soothes, while harsh, overhead, or fluorescent lighting (the worst) increases stress. At home, use less overhead lighting and rely instead on lots of lamps, sconces, and candles. Task lighting can be achieved through the use of recessed cans, pendant lights, or track lighting. Try to use indirect light for accent and also to increase the amount of ambient light in a room without flipping on the overhead and casting a uniform pall over the entire room. Bookcase lighting, under-cabinet lighting, lights in plants, floor lamps, torchières, large table lamps, and small accent lights can all be used to add light and drama to any room. Install dimmer switches so you can control the amount of overhead light you use.

While soft light is relaxing, it is also flattering as well. It softens wrinkles, smoothes lines, and enlarges pupils—a nonverbal sign of openness and warmth. But wait, it gets better: soft, ambient light also does a great job of hiding a thin veneer of dust that may be residing on your furniture. If you haven't dusted lately, turn the lights down!

Make regular use of your fireplace, if you have one and don't live in Houston or Tucson. Consider installing ceramic gas logs; they're clean and easy to use, so having a roaring, crackling fire on chilly nights isn't a big, ashy deal. Alternatively, you can use decorative candle holders to display an array of delicately flickering tea lights inside the fireplace in lieu of a big fire. You'll have all of the romance and none of the mess.

Chapter Two

CLUTTER CONTROL

There is tremendous freedom in the realization that "less is more." Having fewer material possessions, getting rid of the baggage that accumulates in a life, is liberating. Once you tackle an overstuffed closet, for example, and sell or give away the things you haven't used or worn in years, you begin to feel a sense of lightness...of freedom.

But before you tackle the issue of clutter in your home, it helps to have an understanding of *why* the extra baggage is there in the first place. People who live with clutter typically fall into one of three categories.

Understanding your particular "clutter style" and the reasons behind it will help you deal with the fundamental issues. If the underlying reasons behind the clutter in your life and in your home aren't resolved, then you can get rid of every ounce of clutter in your home but it's only a matter of time before it returns.

What's Your Clutter Style?

Chances are good that you fall into one of three clutter styles: the Collector, the Accumulator, or the Prudent Possessor. Take the following quiz to help determine your particular style:

1. If someone asked to see your high school yearbooks, you would:
   (a) know exactly where they are,
   (b) not have a clue about where they are, though you know you still have them around here *somewhere*,
   (c) have a general idea of where they are but it may take a while to find them.

2. What do you do with old magazines?
   (a) keep them in magazine storage containers sorted by title and date,
   (b) toss them in indiscriminate piles anywhere there's space,
   (c) stash them in baskets or in neat piles, then throw them away once they are *really* old.

3. Your collections consist of:
   (a) sequential plates or figurines that may someday be worth something,
   (b) anything and everything under the sun,
   (c) belongings that have been passed down through the generations, although you don't know exactly what belonged to whom.

4. Your photo collection may best be described as:
   (a) neat and orderly, with most of your photos already in albums,
   (b) haphazard—you have photos strewn all over the house,
   (c) ready to be organized—most of your photos are in boxes, ready to be put into albums when you find the time.

5. If you need to find a pen, you:
   (a) know right where to go,
   (b) have them scattered all over the house,
   (c) have a few in every drawer, but many of them don't work.

6. What do you do with clothes you or your children have outgrown?
   (a) clean them and store them in well-marked containers,
   (b) cram them into closets and drawers, where they fill every nook and cranny,
   (c) stash them in storage boxes, just in case you need them someday.

7. Your kitchen can best be described as:
   (a) full of organized tools and cooking gadgets,
   (b) a disaster zone filled with dirty pots and pans, stacks of papers, and piles of stuff,
   (c) filled to the brim with ancient pots, pans, and gadgets, in no discernible order.

8. How many "junk drawers" do you have in your kitchen?
   (a) one or two,
   (b) every drawer is a junk drawer,
   (c) you have some junk in every drawer.

9. How would you best describe your garage?
   (a) full but organized,
   (b) a maze of tools, unmarked boxes, gear, lawn equipment, and trash,

   (c) you've never met a tool or garden gadget you didn't like
        (and keep).

10. When unexpected visitors show up at your doorstep, you:
   (a) are genuinely glad to see them and invite them in without a
        second thought,
   (b) pretend you aren't home,
   (c) are mortified at the mess but invite them in anyway.

How did you score? Give yourself one point for every A, two points for
every B, and three points for every C answer.

If you scored 10–15, you are a *Collector*. Collectors have many possessions, but they are organized and keep everything in some semblance of order.

If you scored 16–24, you are an *Accumulator*. Accumulators keep
everything and have trouble throwing anything away.

If you scored 25 or higher, you are a *Prudent Possessor*. Prudent Possessors are indecisive and keep things because they think they may be
useful some day.

Let's explore these three clutter types in more detail.

COLLECTORS

Collectors often start their collecting habits at an early age. Those who
avidly collected baseball cards, bottle caps, or Cabbage Patch dolls as children often grow up to accumulate "grown-up" collectibles as adults.

Collectors are attracted to the concept of having in their possession
a large number of potentially valuable objects. Numbered collections,
or collections that are added to each year, such as holiday village sets,
commemorative plates, or annually produced figurines or dolls may all
be seen as desirable to Collectors.

Problems arise when the collections become troublesome, either to
the Collector or to other family members. Maintaining and adding to

collections gets expensive, and then there is the not-insignificant issue of where to put things. Keeping the collections clean and free of dust is an issue. And then there is the addictive quality of many collectibles: a hard-core Collector may reach the point where their collecting becomes a type of addiction. Family and finances may suffer as a result.

One woman from Lake Dallas, Texas, had such a compulsion to collect that she eventually rented a storage unit where she could store her collections. She spent so much on figurines and plates that she lost her house and had to move in with her adult daughter, but she kept buying collectibles. Her daughter wouldn't allow them into her house, so the poor woman would take her treasures straight to the storage unit.

Why the compulsion to collect?

On a simple level, psychologists tell us that people collect things to impose order on a chaotic world. Obsessive collectors often lead lives filled with chaos. Psychologists speculate that people subconsciously collect the things they are missing in their lives: train enthusiasts may feel as though they lack power and direction; stamp collectors may lack an ability to communicate; toy collectors feel as though a part of their childhood was somehow lacking.

Understanding the psychological basis for the urge to collect can help a compulsive collector come to terms with his psychological needs. Taking steps to remedy the underlying issues can help free a person mentally from very strong urges to collect.

This is not to say that collecting plates or figurines is a sign of a mental weakness or deficiency. But if your urge to collect has reached the point where it inconveniences you or annoys others, then it may be time to reevaluate this aspect of your life, and maybe even see a counselor who can help you find other ways of meeting certain psychological needs.

ACCUMULATORS

Accumulators are closely related to Collectors in that they have a powerful need to surround themselves with belongings, but this is where the similarities end. At the extreme, Accumulators tend to hoard items of little apparent value, such as old newspapers, empty milk jugs, or cereal boxes. Accumulators have trouble throwing things away. Anything. They keep it all.

Typical items collected by Accumulators may include the following:

- ✦ Newspapers
- ✦ Food storage containers or packing materials
- ✦ Junk mail and catalogs
- ✦ Empty cans and bottles
- ✦ Empty containers for personal care products, such as shampoo or hair spray

Some Accumulators feel the urge to collect living things, such as cats or dogs. In most instances the Accumulator who collects pets has an overriding need to "rescue" these poor animals and is unable to objectively see that the pets typically aren't treated well under these types of conditions.

Psychologists speculate that the urge to accumulate to this degree may have its roots in a childhood or early adulthood marred by lack and deprivation. In some cases their parents compulsively threw things away, which left their offspring with a fear of loss and impermanence. Accumulators mentally attach significance to the items they hoard, seeing value in abundance, even if the items they are collecting have no intrinsic value.

Obsessive accumulating has also been linked to Attention Deficit Disorder and Obsessive-Compulsive Disorder. With ADD, a person may do anything to avoid such mundane tasks as filing papers or putting away folded clothes, so the items pile up in stacks around them. Someone with OCD may feel a compulsion to be surrounded by stacks or piles of belongings, finding comfort in the sheer quantity of possessions.

In the cases where the urge to accumulate truly is compulsive, then medication or cognitive-behavioral therapy can literally solve the problem. When the problem is less severe, it may, ironically, be even more difficult to overcome. Without a behavioral psychologist or medication that restores an unbalanced brain chemistry, dealing with the problem becomes more of an exercise of awareness, discipline, and motivation.

Here is one consideration that may prompt a borderline Accumulator to get rid of the useless items he or she has been accumulating: There may be significant value in large quantities of recyclable materials. Swapping "trash for cash," and freeing up lots of physical and emotional space in the process, can be liberating.

While those who fill their living spaces with items that others see as useless are an extreme, many of us have Accumulator tendencies in just one or two areas. For example, a person may have trouble throwing away cardboard boxes, rationalizing that they have value (*after all*, the reasoning goes, *stores sell them*). Someone else may have an entire drawer filled with rubber bands or paperclips.

In these situations, the person doing the accumulating typically doesn't realize that their holding on to these items can be counterproductive. Large quantities of cardboard boxes, for example, attract roaches and silverfish, and they tend to get dusty; they lose appeal as storage containers when they are filled with bugs and covered with dust, so why keep them around? Keep a few, and get rid of the rest. Similarly, drawers filled with rubber bands or paperclips are probably underutilized. Unless you have too many drawers in your house (and not many of us do), throw away all but a handful and free up that valuable drawer space.

PRUDENT POSSESSORS

If you have trouble throwing or giving things away because you may need them "someday," then welcome to the Prudent Possessors Club.

Prudent Possessors hang on to things for a variety of reasons:

- ✦ I may need this someday.
- ✦ My spouse/son/daughter/Great Aunt Nelda may need this someday.

✦ It can be fixed.

✦ I paid a lot for it.

✦ Someday it may be worth something.

✦ It used to belong to my grandmother.

✦ It's a family heirloom.

✦ It used to belong to a now-deceased relative, although I can't remember who.

✦ It may come back into style.

✦ I have lots of fond memories associated with the item.

✦ It will be wearable again when I lose weight.

✦ My grandmother made it.

✦ I put a lot of work into making it.

✦ I may make something out of it one day.

✦ My kids might want it someday for their own children.

✦ It was a gift.

✦ It's too good to throw out.

Prudent Possessors run into trouble when the things they hang on to ex-
ceed their home's storage capacity. It's fine to keep things as long as
there's plenty of storage space, but once that space is filled, if the Prudent
Possessor continues amassing items that may one day be of use, then the
storage space becomes more and more cramped. Things are packed in to
the point where it becomes impossible to see or even remember what is
there. First drawers, then cabinets, then closets, and finally entire rooms
can become claustrophobic and uncomfortable. In a very literal sense, in
this situation there is too much of a good thing (or things).

Prudent Possessors will find it useful to ask themselves these two
questions as they cull through their belongings and decide what to keep
and what to throw out or give away:

1. Have I used or worn this item in the past two years?

2. If I needed to, could I buy another?

Prudent Possessors will be liberated when they understand that items don't always add value—in fact, sometimes they *keep you from having something valuable*: an orderly, clutter-free home. We'll examine this concept in more detail later, but for now consider that our lives include a revolving door of possessions. We need/want/wear certain things at certain points in our lives, and what works at one point may not work at another. Letting go of the items that have outgrown their usefulness to us is a hallmark sign of someone who controls their possessions, and is not controlled *by them*.

Reduction Strategies for Prudent Possessors

For a large collection that is no longer useful but that holds special memories, *keep one or two pieces, then give away or sell the rest.*

Susan R. inherited a large collection of antique plates from her grandmother. She used the plates once. Now, 15 years later, the plates languish in several boxes in Susan's attic. She doesn't have room for them on her kitchen shelves, but once or twice a year, as she stumbles through the attic looking for Easter baskets or Christmas decorations, Susan runs across the boxes of plates and remembers her wonderful grandmother.

A better option for Susan might be keeping a portion of the collection and giving away or selling the rest. If she kept a service for four or six, instead of twelve, she would free up lots of storage space, and the collection would actually be of a more manageable size, so she would be more likely to use the plates upon occasion. One box would be more user-friendly than several boxes.

Alternatively, Susan could keep just a few pieces of the collection and display them in her home, where she could see the items frequently and enjoy the memories they invoke. She doesn't have to have a dinner party for 12 served on antique china to remember her grandmother; the same memories can be stirred by a single plate.

Another strategy for dealing with items that have outgrown their usefulness is to *take pictures*. Got a mammoth bear-skin rug rolled up and stashed under the bed? Roll it out, take a picture, then get rid of it. You can do the same thing with three-dimensional children's artwork, furnishings you no longer need, and outgrown toys or stuffed animals. Don't dry or press flowers from a once-beautiful bouquet or flower arrangement: take a picture instead. Pictures are smaller, easier to store, and have the ability to invoke the exact same memories as their larger, 3D counterparts.

Here's a tip for families: Scan children's artwork into your computer and keep an electronic file of their masterpieces. This isn't to say that you don't keep some of their work, but, for heaven's sake, don't try to keep it *all*.

Another effective tool for Prudent Possessors to use when winnowing down their piles of stuff is to *write down the memories*. Buy a blank journal and use it exclusively for memories. If you are hanging on to a tacky green vase because it reminds you of your trip to Ireland in 1975, take a few moments to write down the highlights of the trip, the things you remember the most. What did you do there, what did you see that made an impression, what did you enjoy about the adventure? Writing down these memories will serve two purposes: it will help jog your memory as you get older even more than the green vase would have, and it will serve as a written record for generations to come, who would otherwise not attach any meaning to the green vase at all.

You can even combine two strategies and create a scrapbook where you include pictures of the objects as well as a description of the memories they invoke. Do this even for the items you keep, so future generations will understand the significance of the items.

If you enjoy having family snapshots and portraits on display around your home, one strategy is to rotate the collection. For example, framed photos of family and friends can be a charming addition to any décor, but many of us—myself included—find it difficult to replace old pictures with new, so we just keep adding to the collection. If you regularly frame every school picture of every child in your extended family, for example, then the result is an overwhelming array of photos—too many to look at and appreciate, and lots of frames that need to be cleaned and dusted regularly.

The solution? Pick a few old favorites, then rotate the rest. Keep scrapbooks where you can safely store those wonderful photos (more on this to follow). It's okay if they aren't all on display, cluttering your bookshelves or encroaching on every inch of available wall space.

PHOTOGRAPH STORAGE

Anyone who takes a lot of pictures knows how easy it is to be overwhelmed by the result: boxes of photos and negatives, or thousands of photo files, that need to be organized and stored.

There are several effective solutions, depending on the photos you take. If you rely on an old-fashioned camera with film, consider storing your photos and negatives in labeled, acid-free photo-storage boxes. The negatives can be stored in the boxes along with the photos, or they can be stored separately. For irreplaceable photos, consider storing the negatives in a separate place, such as a safety deposit box, a fireproof safe, or a photo-safe box that you keep at a family member's house.

The advent of digital cameras has opened up a whole new world for shutterbugs. Now, instead of taking 12 or 24 or 36 photos, you can take hundreds at a time, without the cost of film or processing.

The result, however, can be overwhelming. What do you do with thousands of photos of your dog or children or your trip to Spain?

The answer is deceptively simple: Photo-management software, or online photo management services, can make the excessive-photo headache go away.

My personal favorite is www.Ofoto.com; www.ClubPhoto.com is another good one. These services allow you to upload and store your photos in easy-to-use, organized folders. You can e-mail individual photos or albums to others, order enlargements, or customize items such as mugs, t-shirts, holiday cards, or calendars emblazoned with your photos.

Incidentally, these sites work with both types of cameras: You can upload digital files, or you can mail your film to them and your photos will be online a couple of days later.

An added benefit of going digital is the fact that you only print the photos you want to keep. Out of fifty photos, or a hundred, or a thousand, for that matter, you may choose to print only a few. So while you have a digital record of many, many images, the actual paper trail, the hard-copy photos you'll want to organize and store and maybe put into a scrapbook, are quite manageable.

When I relied on film, I used to fill one or two photo boxes *a year* with family pictures. Now that I've gone digital, I have only the really good, "keeper" photos printed; the collection of photos that I have to manage has become much smaller, and all the printed photos are good enough to go into the family scrapbook.

Specialty software opens up vast new options for digital photos and video files, too. Photos and slideshows can be put on CDs; music can be added. Digital video clips can be stored and organized. Other software sites to check out include www.ArcSoft.com and www.Photo Meister.com.

The right software and a high-quality printer does away with the need for such a service, although, if you manage your photos yourself, you will probably need some type of an organizational system to keep the files manageable. Some choose to store their photos chronologically; others organize by subject matter. The type of system you choose doesn't matter; the keys to remember are *simplicity* and *consistency*.

A good source of photo-management equipment, by the way, is Light Impressions (www.LightImpressionsDirect.com). This company sells everything you need to keep your photos, negatives, slides, and CDs clean, organized, and protected.

Determining Your Clutter Ratio

The Finnish press reported an interesting study in which an art student decided, for her thesis, to take inventory of every object in her home. Using traditional archeological methods, she discovered she owned 6,126 items. Then she analyzed her possessions based on how often she used them. Here is her tally:

Objects never used: 1,457

Objects used less than once a year: 2,209

Objects used once or twice a year: 1,411

Objects used every month: 587

Objects used every week: 401

Objects used every day: 61

An analysis of her data revealed that 24 percent of the objects in her home were never used and a further 59 percent were used only once or twice a year. Of the remaining 17 percent, only 1 percent of the objects she owned were used every day.

Assuming that this art student wasn't an obsessive-compulsive pack rat, it's fairly safe to assume that many of us also fall into the trap of owning far more than we need or even want. The trick lies in holding on to only those possessions that are truly meaningful or useful. You can get rid of the rest.

The Essential Bookshelf

For those who have a tendency towards accumulating clutter, bookshelves are wonderful but potentially dangerous things. Nothing stores books, knickknacks, and photos as efficiently as a well-planned, well-organized bookshelf. On the other hand, bookshelves beg, "Here I am with all these nice, flat surfaces; load me up!"

Professional decorators know a few tricks to make bookshelves aesthetically appealing. Here are a few tips:

✦ Give your eyes a place to rest. Unless the bookshelf is literally in your home library, leave some empty, uncluttered space.

✦ Vary the contents. Break the visual monotony. Add a small silk plant here, a photo there.

✦ Align all the books together close to the edge of the shelf. When the books are crammed back against the wall and the outer row is ragged, the end result looks messy and unkempt.

✦ Group books together by subject.

✦ Unless you really will reread them, get rid of paperbacks you've already read. Take them to a used book store; although they only pay cents on the dollar, you can use the money to buy a book or two you haven't already read. Or take them to a nearby hospital waiting room. Or sell them online.

✦ Use upright magazine containers to store magazines; they are available in office-supply stores.

✦ If your bookshelves are still crowded, cull through them periodically and give away or sell the books you have already read and are unlikely to reread—even hardbacks. What's the use of a stagnant, crowded collection of thoughts and ideas you've already considered? Keep only your favorites.

Training Your Eye to Spot Clutter

Make it a habit to train your eye to look at a room objectively. Take a step back and survey the area. What is not needed? What is adding visual clutter? Viewing a room objectively takes practice. We quickly become accustomed to our surroundings and lose perspective.

There is a fine line between tasteful accessories and visual clutter. The fallout from years of random accumulation adds up. A stash of papers here, an unused planter there, a figurine inherited from an aunt, an unused picture frame…these seemingly harmless items multiply and then coalesce into a smothering avalanche of *stuff*.

Once you develop and then hone the ability to look at a room objectively, you may be mortified by what you finally see. Random, meaningless stuff is *everywhere*! You didn't collect these things overnight, and you won't solve the problem of too much clutter overnight, either.

How, then, to remedy this situation?

In many cases the areas of clutter and chaos are concentrated. These "hot spots" are default zones, places we put things when we don't know where else to put them. You want to start by gaining control of your hot spots.

Shelves and bookcases—or any flat surface, for that matter—are prime accumulation areas. Look at your desk, for example. Are there items on the desktop that serve no good purpose, that don't even have sentimental value? If so, clear them off. Get rid of them. Keep only the items that are genuinely useful or that bring a smile to your face. Keep pictures of friends and family; get rid of anything useless or extraneous. Remember our mantra: *If it doesn't make you smile or serve a definite purpose, toss it.*

Know Your Weaknesses

Many of us have a tendency to buy the same types of things again and again. I have a weakness for candles, for example. I love them, but as a result I tend to buy too many. When I cull through my candle collection I toss out votive holders that are chipped or cracked, mismatched, or that I haven't used in over a year. I keep a single drawer for votives and when it's full, I put myself on a self-imposed candle-buying ban. I don't buy more until I've burned the candles I already bought.

What's your weakness? Do you buy too many picture frames? Coffee cups? Collectibles? Shoes? There's nothing wrong with buying things, but the trouble starts when you buy things you don't *need*. This is where clutter begins.

Small Steps

It is all too easy to become completely overwhelmed as you contemplate cleaning and organizing your home. Remember that homes don't become cluttered and disorganized overnight, and they won't be restored to a state of sparkling, organized splendor overnight, either. Outwitting housework is a process, a series of small steps, a fine-tuning (or overhaul) of the way you approach the care and maintenance of your surroundings. What is important to remember is that, as with any area of your life in which you desire change, in order to get different results, you're going to have to do things differently.

Fighting a Compulsion to Collect

As you begin your campaign to reduce clutter, get rid of the least valuable, most replaceable items first. Understand that giving up possessions runs counter to our shopping- and collecting-obsessed culture, which urges us to buy and consume more and more. If you're not used to it, jettisoning things can be difficult at first. So start small, with the easy stuff.

If you have an overwhelming urge to collect, you may need professional help in coming to terms with this psychological need, but this doesn't mean that you can't still make progress in this area outside of the psychologist's office. As with other forms of compulsions, the urge to collect items that others find meaningless can be overcome. Start small.

Start with paper. Begin in one room, in a corner of one room. Make it the most visible room in the house, where your results will be seen and noticed immediately. Set up a large trash can, pop on a pair of plastic gloves (which sends a mental signal that you're dealing with *trash*), and dig in.

What are you looking for? The object here is to throw away anything you don't need. Throw away old newspapers, catalogs, coupons, magazines, flyers, and junk mail. Keep current bills. File old statements. (For more on filing papers and documents, see Chapter 8.) If you have a particularly large pile of paper, don't worry about filing meticulously; a box will do just fine. And, keep in mind that most papers can be replaced.

Some people have an urge to collect items that others would consider to be trash. I've known of people who collected foil pie tins, empty jars and plastic containers, styrofoam meat tray liners, and empty cereal boxes or egg cartons. Discarding these items is easier when you realize that they are replaceable and that they have no intrinsic value. These are not dear old friends, they are acquaintances. Most of them can be taken to the recycling center. Get rid of them.

Clean, Empty Boxes Are Signs from the Universe

Getting rid of things is easier if you have an easy, efficient place to put the items you no longer want. Every time you run across a large, clean, empty cardboard box, use it as a container for items to give away. The Fly Lady, the Internet home cleaning guru from www.FlyLady.net, calls this the "Blessings Box"—this is where you put usable items you and your family no longer need or want, to give to Goodwill or the Salvation Army or other reputable charity organizations, so that others may be blessed. As the Fly Lady notes, giving to others is not only a wonderful way to help *them*; you help yourself as well when you throw pebbles of goodwill into the pond of humanity.

So, whenever you run across a big, empty box, see this as a sign from the universe that it's time to bless others with the things in your house that are adding nothing but clutter. Put the box in a central location and go on a hunt; you are looking for things to fill up the box. Glance around rooms in your house and look for the obvious things first. Once visible surfaces are clear, start opening drawers and cupboards.

The more Blessings Boxes you fill, the more you will begin to feel the lightness of spirit that is brought about by generosity toward others and pared-down, streamlined living areas. The more you give away, the lighter you become.

When you run across a smaller, sturdier box, use it as an opportunity to cull through your books. See these boxes as invitations to clear out space on your bookshelves, which we already know are prime areas for attracting extraneous items and clutter, and used paperbacks certainly fill the bill.

Fling Shui

Once you realize the freedom that comes from ridding your home and your life of excess baggage, you will become more adept at instantly recognizing clutter and getting rid of it.

You can spend a fortune learning the secrets of feng shui, which advocates arranging rooms, furniture, colors, and objects in order to harness the inherent powers that are available with the proper alignment of forms and materials.

Or you can delve into the joys of what the Fly Lady calls *fling shui*, where you harness the inherent power of getting rid of excess baggage in your life. It doesn't cost a thing, but the payoff is tremendous.

Preparing to fling shui consists of realizing that our lives include a constant revolving door of *things*. Pictures, clothes, books, papers, accessories…our home is a repository of all of these types of things.

Think back to the time when you were small. Your room was filled with treasures, with things you loved and valued and cherished. Have you kept all of those things? Probably not. You may have a tattered stuffed animal or box of treasures somewhere, a cherished vestige of childhood, but you didn't keep *everything*.

You'll discover the ability to fling shui when you recognize things that are important to keep and things that are just temporarily passing through your life.

Picture This

Visualizing an example is often helpful in helping you identify clutter. We get so attached to our own stuff that it's hard to see it as extraneous. Consider this example:

Picture a table in front of a light, airy window. Let's put a few things on the table.

Picture a tablecloth, a lamp, a stack of books. Add a candle, a framed picture, and a tiny replica of the Eiffel Tower. The table is getting crowded, but we're not done yet. Add two more framed pictures, a bottle of hand lotion, a box of tissues, a phone, a purse, a coffee cup, and a stack of unread mail. The surface of the table has completely disappeared.

Now, let's clear our table off. Let's put the mail in a special box or basket in the kitchen or home office. The coffee cup goes in the dishwasher, the purse goes in the laundry room or into a chair where it is out of sight, and the tissues and hand lotion go into a nearby drawer or closet. Pick a favorite photo and put the others away. The Eiffel Tower holds no particular memories—it was a gift, but you can't remember who gave it to you. Get rid of it. Finally, unless it's winter and you're consciously adding depth and texture to your surroundings, get rid of the tablecloth. Launder it and hang it in a closet. Dust the lamp.

Now, what do we have left?

A table in front of a light, airy window. On it are a lamp, a framed picture, and a candle. Add a small plant or a crystal vase of cut flowers. The result is a peaceful, serene still life. The streamlined décor and clean surfaces provide a place for the eyes to rest. The clutter has been removed, but the truth is apparent: less is definitely more.

Let's do the mantel next.

Visualize a fireplace with stained-wood trim. Hanging above the mantel is a large, framed picture. On the mantel are a vase, a bowl, a silk plant, three candles, and framed pictures of eight grandchildren.

Oh dear.

Let's clear it off, shall we?

Let's keep the framed picture, a candle, the plant, and let's add a small stack of decorative hardback books. The vase, bowl, candles, and pictures are too much. There's no place for the eyes to rest. Put them away.

It's easy to envision the improvements we've just made in our make-believe trouble spots. The table's all cleared off; the mantel's nice and clean. What's harder is seeing clutter in *your own space*. The objects that fill your home are personal; there's a story behind every single doohickey in your possession.

This is a pack-rat mentality and a way of thinking that must be abandoned post-haste!

The Ultimate Clutter-Busting Strategy: Have a Garage Sale

When clutter and useless household objects threaten to overwhelm, it's time to either call Goodwill or have a garage sale. I like to do both: first I have the garage sale, then I call Goodwill to come pick up what's left.

Having a successful garage sale takes a bit of work and advance preparation, but, in this case, a few hours of work can yield big results.

Before you begin, understand that there is an entire subculture out there of dedicated garage-salers. They get up early every Friday and Saturday and cruise the streets; they devour the weekend papers to find out where the estate sales and garage sales are being held. These *potential buyers* are *looking* for a sale. Make yourself visible to them. Put an ad in the paper, and display several prominent, easy-to-read signs near your house on the day of the sale.

Your signs should be easy to read and should give an address, time of sale, and, if there's room, a few "teaser" comments can be included.

Here's an example of an ineffective sign:

> **Garage Sale**
> **Friday and Saturday**

This one is much better:

MULTIFAMILY GARAGE SALE!
Friday and Saturday, 8–2
193 Elm Street
Toys, Clothes, Books, Movies, CDs!!

Give yourself a week or two to get everything ready. Set aside an area for items to go in the garage sale; the garage is an ideal spot so you won't have to move everything twice.

Call your neighbors and invite them to join forces with you for the sale.

Joining forces with the neighbors is beneficial for several reasons: first, lots of people slowly cruise by garage sales, using eagle eyes to see if there is "anything worth stopping for." Having the accumulated sale items of several families instead of just one greatly increases your odds that these drive-by garage-salers will actually see something they like and stop to browse. Also, garage sales advertised as "multifamily sales" tend to draw more customers for the very same reason: the promise of a wider selection.

What to sell? Anything that is good enough to give to charity. If a charity wouldn't take it, then odds are good that no one will want to buy it, either.

Next, in our marketing-savvy consumer culture, our eyes have been trained to expect *order* and *style* when we shop. Consumers are more likely to stop and seriously consider items for sale that are carefully and artfully arranged, as opposed to items carelessly tossed in a box. Well-displayed items carry with them an aura of value, while boxes and piles of stuff send a strong message of "useless junk." So set up the items in your sale carefully.

Pricing your garage sale items on the low side is another strategy to improve the success of your sale. Colored garage sale price stickers in increments of 10, 25, 50 cents, $1, $5, "make an offer," and so on, can be found in many home- or office-supply stores. If you are having a multi-family sale, use a different color of sticker for each family, to simplify bookkeeping.

Group items together according to price. Everything on one table is 50 cents, for example. Keep your price increments simple. Don't price something at 35 cents, for example. Make it 25 or 50 cents, but not 35.

How long should your sale last? Not too long, or you'll burn out and vow never to do it again. Most potential buyers are out early, looking for bargains, so you can have your sale relatively early and get it over with. Friday and Saturday are the best days, and having the sale from 8 A.M. until noon or 1 or 2 P.M. should give potential buyers plenty of time. If you have joined forces with the neighbors, you can take turns running the sale, so you don't all have to be present the whole time.

To simplify accounting for multi-family sales, use a large legal pad to keep track of sales. You can either write down the price of items sold under the heading of each family, or peel off the price stickers and put them directly on the family's page in the notebook.

Finally, be prepared for early birds. Lots of dedicated garage-salers make it a habit to hit sales before they officially begin. Decide ahead of time if you want to allow early birds or if you want to make them wait. (Since the object is to get rid of stuff, and early birds often are shopping for stores or for their own sales later, I happily let them shop and buy to their heart's content.)

Once the sale is over, cart the leftover items back into your garage and arrange to have Goodwill or another charity pick them up. You can use what you didn't sell as a tax write-off. And your home will now be blissfully, happily, free of junk.

Chapter Three

START IN THE KITCHEN

In many homes the kitchen is the center of the action. This is where families tend to congregate, eat, do homework, sort mail, and just hang out. The kitchen also tends to be a repository for odds and ends, for mail, school papers, backpacks, lunch boxes, and various random items that have no other place to go.

Unfortunately, the kitchen is also a room where lots of things *do* belong. Pots, pans, food items, coffee makers, blenders, toaster ovens, dishwashing dispensers, paper towels, spices, canisters, plants, candles, and kitschy décor items often jockey for limited counter space. The result can be a frenzied melée of stuff. And this is *before* anyone brings in the mail or sets down a sheaf of school papers that need to be signed, filed, or discarded. You've got to tame the kitchen chaos…but where to begin?

Realize the Potential

A clean, organized kitchen sets the tone for the rest of the house. When the kitchen is clean, it really doesn't matter if other areas are in varying states of disarray. The other areas take their cue from the kitchen. Once the kitchen is clutter-free and clean, waves of cosmic clean karma begin wafting through the other rooms.

How does this work? I'm not sure, but in my experience, if my kitchen is clean, my eyes automatically scan other areas in close proximity. I suddenly notice a pile of newspapers scattered beneath the coffee table. My eagle eyes notice a layer of dust on top of the TV armoire; the pillows on the sofa would look much nicer standing at attention, and so it goes. Once the kitchen is clean, the rest of the house seems to fall into place.

On the other hand, if the kitchen is in disarray, then it doesn't matter if the rest of the house is sparkling clean. The house feels dirty. Stacks of unwashed dishes, crumbs and drips on the countertops, a cooktop splattered with grease, countertops piled high with papers and clutter—aaargh!

Clearly, if you want your house to look and feel clean, then the kitchen is the place to start.

Easy Kitchen Décor

I once had an all-white kitchen. It was a nightmare to keep clean. Every crumb showed up like it was lit from above by a Broadway spotlight. The floor was one gigantic cleaning nightmare.

Then we moved. My next kitchen had a gorgeous, gleaming, blond hardwood floor. The countertop was a beige composite material that didn't burn or stain. I could carve a loaf of bread into wafers and the resulting piles of crumbs were all but invisible. It was heaven.

Then we moved again. The next kitchen fell somewhere between its two predecessors on the Ease-of-Cleaning scale. Oak hardwood flooring did a great job of hiding wee bits of dirt and debris on the floor, but plain beige tile countertops were just one step ahead of the all-white formica. Not ideal.

We replaced the beige tiles with a dark, mottled granite, and I was in heaven once again. Crumbs, splatters, coffee drips—all of it disappeared against the granite. In fact, I had to squat down and look at the counter from the side in order to find stuff to clean off. That's how well it camouflaged.

Another easy-décor trick: an undermounted sink. Crumbs and spills and drips whisk straight into the sink instead of catching in the grout or against the edge of the sink.

If you're in the market for kitchen appliances, know that stainless steel appliances may be all the rage, but they are also magnets for fingerprints. In fact, I'm going to write a letter right now to the FBI recommending that they institute a new policy of having crime suspects whip up a dish of whatever in a kitchen with stainless steel appliances. They'll get all the good, complete prints their crime-busting hearts desire. Unless you really love the look, go with black or white appliances instead.

TIP: *Plagued by Fingerprints on Stainless Steel? Try This:*

Caldrea makes an olive oil–based stainless steel cleaner that promises to reduce fingerprints ($12 for 11.8 ounces, 877-576-8808, or www.Caldrea.com).

To keep kitchen cabinets gleaming, Murphy's Oil Soap is the best on the block. This all-purpose wood cleaner safely strips oil and grease from wood surfaces, including sealed wood floors. Because Murphy's also removes wax, however, it should not be used on waxed wood floors. It does a great job, however, on grouted tile floors. Surface grime is removed, and the oil in the cleaner reseals the grout.

Cooktops are another element of most kitchens that can either be relatively easy to clean, or can be nothing short of a nightmare of cooked-on, impossible-to-remove filth. If you have an electric cooktop with coiled heating elements and drip pans and a thousand nooks and crevices, you'll want to adopt a few habits that can help you avoid having to clean the stove.

For example, take great care to not overfill pots and pans as you cook. You don't want things boiling over, onto, and into the nooks and crannies. Use splatter guards. Use the microwave to cook bacon and anything that splatters. I once sautéed a batch of meatballs on my electric cooktop; it took me *forever* to get the darn thing clean again. Now I cover meatballs with foil and bake them in the oven.

With gas cooktops, you are likely to have fewer nooks and crannies to clean, but the hotter temperatures mean that it is more difficult to control potential boil-overs. Cooking with care and making sure you don't overfill pots and pans can go a long way toward thwarting the need to clean your cooktop.

While you're cooking, be sure to take advantage of any and all vents in the kitchen, cooktop vents, downdraft vents—anything that makes any effort at all to remove smoke- and grease-laden air. It may make a bit of noise, but turn that fan on high as you cook and you'll save yourself clean-up later.

What about the oven? Don't spend a fortune on oven cleaners. Spend your money on aluminum foil instead. Use baking dishes with lids. Cover things before you bake them. Use foil to line cookie sheets that you can then place beneath potentially messy casseroles.

What about big things, like turkeys, you ask? You may have to be creative. I use a big turkey pan with high sides that allows the bird to rest down in the pan. The turkey browns quite nicely, and most of the splatters are contained.

These *preventive-maintenance skills* are a vital part of outwitting housework in the kitchen. Use plastic wrap or paper towels to cover foods as they heat in the microwave. Use disposable foil liners beneath burners. If something spills and then burns, all you have to do is throw away the liner.

The trick is to learn to cook with cleaning in mind. Using nonstick sprays, covering things before baking, using splatter guards, and so on are all ways of making life easier for yourself once the meal is through. (While you're busy covering casseroles or other items that might splatter before you put them in the oven, go an extra step and spray the inside of the foil with nonstick cooking spray, so it won't stick to the food it's covering.)

Clean as You Go

As you cook, the trick to keeping your kitchen in order is simple: you have to train yourself to *clean as you go*. Years of bad kitchen habits can be hard to break, but the task of changing a throw-caution-to-the-wind-as-you-cook mindset will be much easier once you realize that a little bit of effort as you go saves a lot of effort in the end. What it takes is a bit of focus and determination.

Kitchens are traps for those who are neatness-challenged because they are filled with distracting landmines. Cleaning as you go is challenging because it requires an additional awareness, but don't worry; this awareness is not difficult to develop.

What this means is that as you cook, you are aware of your actions. You keep a trash can within easy reach and throw things away as you go instead of putting them on the counter to throw away later. You start off with an empty dishwasher so you can load it as you go. You wipe up spills and splats as soon as they occur. You rinse and reuse pots and pans, so after cooking a big meal you may have one or two pots to clean instead of four or five. You consolidate where you can, conserving space and energy, reusing utensils, looking for shortcuts and tricks to outwit the mess.

This conservation of energy can manifest itself in small ways. For example, when I cook spaghetti, I have one pot of simmering sauce and another pot of cooking pasta. When I stir the sauce, I am left with a drippy, sauce-covered spoon that will make a mess wherever I put it down. So I stir the sauce and then stir the noodles. The boiling water rinses off my sauce spoon and it's clean before I put it in the spoon rest. I know, I know, this is a small thing, but when you are cooking you can look for lots of small shortcuts like this, and the cumulative effect is to make cleanup much easier.

TIP: *A Tip from the Pros*

In the morning, coffee accoutrements can make a big mess, so take a cue from Starbucks and pour creamer, sweetener, or flavorings into the cup *before* you add the coffee. The pouring coffee will blend with the flavorings, and you will be spared a countertop covered with drippy spoons.

Preemptive Menu Planning

Another way to minimize the mess? *Preemptive menu planning.* This is a great way to minimize the time you spend cleaning your kitchen. Here's how it works:

Consider your old method. Let's say that your first impulse is to prepare a nice, big breakfast. Here's the old, messy menu, and then the new menu designed with easy cleanup in mind:

Old menu: scrambled eggs, bacon, fruit salad, and toasted bagels.

New menu: breakfast casserole, low-fat sausage, sliced apples or bananas, and toast.

Not much of a difference, you say? Maybe not at first glance, but look a little bit closer. The casserole can be made the night before, then popped in the oven as you start to prepare the meal. Another benefit:

any leftovers can stay in the pan, which will reduce cleanup (one dirty pan, two or more meals). The low-fat sausage cooks much cleaner than bacon and is healthier, too. A sliced apple or banana is much less messy to prepare and eat than seeding, peeling, and dicing a medley of fruits. And bread (for toast) usually comes presliced, which will keep wayward bagel crumbs off the counter. All of these minor details add up to a cleaner kitchen in the end, which means less work for you.

Quick-Fix Supplies to Keep in the Kitchen

- ✓ Clorox Disinfecting Wipes: for all hard, nonwood surfaces. The wipes are easy to use and they leave a clean, fresh scent.
- ✓ Windex Glass and Surface Wipes: work great on windows and chrome.
- ✓ Microfiber cloths such as StarFiber (www.StarFibers.com): very effective for polishing stainless steel.
- ✓ Clorox ReadyMop: mop the floor quickly and easily—without a bucket.
- ✓ Swiffer: the ultimate crumb- and dust-buster. The Swiffer product is relatively new on the cleaning scene. These electromagnetically charged cloths can either be attached to a special type of duster and used to "sweep" floors, or the cloths can be used for hand dusting. Either way, they do a great job of collecting dust, dirt, and hair.

Develop Good Cleaning Habits

All of us have habits. Happily, once you break an old habit and replace it with something new, the new habit becomes just as automatic as the old one was.

Maybe your old after-dinner habit, for example, is to set dirty dishes all over the counter, filling every available space. The dirty plates, cutlery, and glasses co-mingle with empty containers, used cooking utensils, and crusty pots and pans. Oh, the chaos!

How to break this habit? Begin by making a new habit of preemptive dishwashing.

As you cook, rinse and stack items to be washed to the left of the sink, like with like. Once a pot or pan has been used, fill it immediately with hot, soapy water. Never let food harden on a used pan. Let things soak.

Once you have a dirty pot or bowl, fill it with hot, soapy water and put it in the sink. Toss dirty utensils into the soapy water as you use them, to soak. Once the meal is over, used knives, forks, and spoons go there too.

I keep a clean, dry dish towel spread out to the right of the sink as I cook. Once I use a utensil, I slip it into the hot water to soak or put it straight into the dishwasher. If I plan on using it again I rinse it off and put it on the clean towel. Either way, the utensil is ready to be either used again or cleaned, but it is not sitting on a countertop forming an impermeable crust of hardened food.

Deal with debris immediately. Never set a piece of trash down on the counter. If it's trash, put it directly into the garbage. *Once the meal is over,* empty glasses and cups first and put them in the dishwasher, or wash them and put them in the dish drainer. Scrape leftovers into the trash or disposal, rinse plates using a heavy-duty scrub brush, then put them directly into the dishwasher or dish drainer. At this point, don't stack them up to load them later. Do it now, and cut out this middle step.

Once the dishes are done, clear off the table. Pick up place mats, and put the salt and pepper and other condiments back into the cupboard or pantry. Get rid of every indication that a meal was had at the table. Clear it off completely.

Now, the table and the counters are clear. Take a damp kitchen rag and wipe the table clean, then spritz it with a grease-cutting all-purpose cleaner and wipe down all the kitchen surfaces, paying special attention to the counters and cooktop and around the sink.

CLEAN COOKING STRATEGIES

So, now you know a quick, efficient way to clean a totally trashed kitchen, but you can avoid the pain—or at least some of it—by using other strategies to minimize the mess that is made in the first place. Here are a few ideas:

+ **Cook outside.** Cooking outside saves cleaning inside. Cook the entire meal outside! I frequently toss some seasoned chicken breasts or fish on the grill, add a big foil pouch of vegetables, maybe cook some rice inside, and dinner's done.

+ **Use a crock pot.** Invest in a good cookbook for the crock pot and watch your dinner woes melt away. There is a real beauty in tossing a few ingredients in a pot, going away for a few hours, and returning to a house that smells wonderful and a dinner that is ready to serve. An added bonus? Cleanup is a cinch.

+ **Use cooking bags.** Cooking bags have all the advantages of crock-pot cooking, but they're faster. If you have an hour or two before dinner, pop your ingredients in the bag, put it in the oven, then go do something else—pay bills or clean out a desk drawer or do a load of laundry or take a walk. Dinner is cooking itself.

+ **Cook once...eat twice.** This is a cardinal rule in my house. For every big, elaborate dish I prepare, I get *at least* two meals out of my effort. If I make soup, I make a lot of it. My casseroles are enormous. Why go to all the trouble for just one meal?

+ **Eat out.** If you just can't bear the thought of cooking and then cleaning, then take advantage of the local restaurant, diner, or fast food joint and give yourself a break.

+ **Delegate.** In some families the rule is that the person who cooks doesn't have to clean up the kitchen afterwards. Others delegate certain meals or days of the week to certain family members. If you have older kids or teenagers in the house, this can be a great way to help them learn about and contribute to the effort that goes into food preparation and cleanup.

The Rubber Glove Trick

Once the meal is over, pop on a pair of rubber gloves. This serves many purposes. It keeps your hands and fingernails protected, obviously, but it also sends a signal to your brain: "Now it's time to clean the kitchen." You won't be easily distracted when the rubber gloves are on—you can't do anything else. You can't notice and then leaf through a stack of mail with your rubber gloves on. The gloves also send a signal to your family: it's time to clean the kitchen. Whoever's wearing the gloves is unavailable to play Monopoly or help with homework. The gloves mean business.

I find that when I'm wearing my lovely yellow rubber gloves I clean up the kitchen about three times faster than when I'm bare-handed. I don't hesitate to plunge right into washing a sticky bowl or grease-covered frying pan.

Shameless Product Endorsement #1:

DAWN POWER DISSOLVER

I spend a lot of time cruising store aisles in search of products that can make my life easier. I find a lot of newfangled items that just look like good places to throw away money, but every so often I run across a truly ingenious product that I just have to take home and try.

So it was with great joy that I stumbled upon Power Dissolver by Dawn. The bold promise made by this dishwashing upstart? *No scrubbing.* I decided to put it to the test.

First I tried the product as recommended: on dried-up, baked-on, difficult-to-remove food remnants stuck to the bottom of a baking pan.

Squirt squirt, wait 10 minutes, and the promise was that the food would wash or wipe right off. It did.

So I brought out the big gun: an old, well-loved, much-used wok with 10 years' worth of oily glop stuck to the base. (The electric mechanism can't be immersed in water, so I had yet to find a suitable way to clean the darn thing.) As long as the part that actually touched food was clean, I reasoned.... But the oily glop still bothered me, on the rare occasions when I flipped the wok over and scratched my head in befuddlement about how to clean it.

So, drum roll, please. Did it work? You bet it did. It took two applications, as the bottle said it might, but the greasy, caked-on black stuff wiped right off.

What's in this product, you ask? Battery acid. Not really. Well, maybe. The ingredients listed are vague "biodegradable alkaline cleaning agents and solvents." I suspect that it's a liquid form of oven cleaner—a convenient, directable spray instead of a coat-everything-in-sight foam. But the bottom line is that this stuff works.

HOW TO OUTWIT REALLY STUBBORN POTS

If food is baked or scalded onto a pot, try the "pot boiler" trick: fill the pot halfway with sudsy water and bring the water to a boil. The cooked-on food will lift right off with a spoon or spatula.

Another effective solution for removing hardened food remnants is heavy-duty oven cleaner (or Dawn Power Dissolver; see box). Spray it on and let it sit for 10–15 minutes. The softened gunk will wipe off easily.

A Zen Approach to Dishwashing

I used to hate washing dishes. It wasn't that I just didn't much like it; I really *detested* the task. I hated getting my hands wet and dirty. I hated the slimy feel of diluted leftovers. Above all, I hated the fact that the running water kept me from hearing and participating in family discussions. The whole process felt icky and isolating. And then I read something that changed my mind.

Washing dishes can be relaxing, a small retreat after preparing and then consuming a meal. The process of washing dishes incorporates several elements: warm water, repetitive motion, and the soothing sounds of running water. Once I popped on a good pair of rubber gloves, which insulated my hands from the slimy feel I hate, I learned to view the process as a chance to immerse myself in a warm, sudsy world of peace and calm and soothing repetitive motion.

This change in perspective worked wonders for how I approach cleaning up a messy kitchen. Now it's my favorite room of the house to clean. I choose to look at it as a mini-escape, a chance to be alone for a few moments with my thoughts. It is truly amazing how such a minor attitude tweak can revolutionize a job you despise.

The Secret Life of Sponges

Used kitchen sponges may look serviceable, but the microscopic fact is that they are *really* gross. Toss them in the garbage post-haste and replace them with something sanitary, like a sturdy scrub brush that can be washed every time you run the dishwasher.

I keep one sponge in my kitchen that I use for one purpose: it is a nonscratching abrasive number that I use to clean my porcelain sink. I use it in conjunction with an abrasive cleanser—I like Barkeeper's Friend—and I only use it once all visible food remnants have been safely washed down the drain. Once the sink is scrubbed, I rinse the sponge with hot, soapy water, squeeze it out, then put it in a plastic bowl beneath the sink to dry. I still wouldn't be too jazzed to find out what microscopic friends my sponge harbors—just think of the colonies of slime that could thrive in a food-filled, wet...well, it's just too gross to even contemplate.

SHINY SINK KNOW-HOW

The kitchen sink is one of those places—like the bathroom—that begs to be cleaned well and often. You can make the job easier with these tips:

✦ Scratched enamel sinks respond best to an energetic scrub with a sponge and an abrasive cleanser. Stainless steel sinks are easier to clean: once you've done the dishes and the sink is empty, simply squirt an all-purpose cleanser like 409 on the sink and faucet then wipe dry with a damp kitchen towel.

✦ If you have a rubber mat in the bottom of the sink, once a week or so fill the sink with hot water then add a cup of Clorox bleach to the water. Toss in any scrub brushes or sponges as well to disinfect the whole lot.

✦ If you have tile or grout around the kitchen sink, use a toothbrush, rag, or sponge soaked with the Clorox solution to remove crumbs, mold, and mildew.

✦ The secret to having a really shiny, sparkly sink is to rinse it out and *dry it* with an absorbent dish towel once you're finished with the dishes. The dish towel removes water spots and really makes the sink and faucet gleam.

The Beauty of Cheap, Teflon-Coated Pans

Here's my vote for Teflon as one of the great inventions of the 20th century. A Teflon-coated pan can ease cleanup like nothing else. But buy your Teflon wisely.

I once made the mistake of buying an expensive Teflon-coated pan. Years later, once the coating was long gone, I still hung on to the expensive pan, because I paid a small fortune for it. What a waste. Now I buy cheap pans and toss them once the coating begins to fail. If you use a Teflon-coated pan often, the reality is that the coating doesn't last forever. A few scratches inflicted by a metal spatula from a well-meaning "helper" or an accidental ride in the dishwasher can ruin the slick surface quickly. So buy them cheap and buy them often.

10 Tips for an Uncluttered Kitchen

1. Clean off the countertops. Get rid of knickknacks and appliances you rarely use.

2. Give away pots, pans, containers, and utensils that you never use.

3. Use drawer organizers to keep cooking utensils separate and easy to find.

4. Store like with like. Keep all cleaning supplies in one place, all spices on one shelf, all baking supplies together. This simple rule will help keep your kitchen streamlined and organized.

5. Store things efficiently, near where they will be used. Put coffee cups in the shelf over the coffee maker, for example, and put cooking utensils in a drawer by the cooktop.

6. Utilize the backs of cabinet doors for storage—a rack for spice jars, for example. The back of the cabinet door beneath the sink is a great place for installing a small storage rack to keep cleaning products and supplies convenient yet out of sight.

7. Use a vertical organizer in a cabinet near the oven to store cookie sheets and other baking supplies that tend to slide around haphazardly when stored flat.

8. If you can never find a chip clip when you need one, purchase a whole bag of plastic clothes pins instead. The handy clips are inexpensive, durable, abundant, and can be used to seal just about any bag in the kitchen, including partially used bags of frozen foods and plastic cereal box liners.

9. Keep your refrigerator door free of clutter. Post lists and important phone numbers on the inside of a cabinet door, instead.

10. When you wash dishes and pots by hand, dry them and put them away immediately. Even if you don't wipe them dry, dishes rinsed in hot water will dry in minutes upside down in a drainer, so eliminate visual clutter and put them away.

10 Tips for a Sparkling Kitchen

1. Add 1/4 cup vinegar along with dishwashing detergent when washing dishes. The vinegar cuts grease and makes dishes sparkle.

2. Sprinkle spills in the oven with salt. Once the spill cools, the food remnants and salt will brush away easily.

3. Lay a thick, grooved, rubber mat in the cabinet beneath the kitchen sink. One day the sink will leak, and you will break your arm patting yourself on the back when the thick rubber mat contains the mess.

4. Keep a supply of paper plates on hand for days when you'd really rather not have to wash a bunch of dishes.

5. Stock up on refrigerator-to-oven bakeware. You can bake, serve, and then store food all in one container.

6. To clean a coffee grinder, put dry white rice in the chamber and grind away.

7. To clean a blender, rinse it, fill halfway with hot water and a squeeze of dishwashing liquid, then turn it on for 15–30 seconds. Rinse well, dry, and put away.

8. Wipe down counters and your cook top frequently, which will keep crumbs and minor spills and splatters at bay.

9. Rinse and reuse pots and pans as you cook instead of reaching for a clean new pot every time.

TIP: *Killing Two Birds...*

If your coffee pot gets grungy and stained, fill halfway with hot water, then add 2 cups white vinegar. Run through a cycle. Next, pour a cup of baking soda down the kitchen drain, and then, when the vinegar solution has run through the coffee pot, pour the hot solution down the drain. Let sit for 10 minutes. Both your coffee pot and the kitchen sink will be clean. (If stains remain in the coffee pot, put the carafe in the top rack of the dishwasher and run through a cycle after the vinegar treatment, or, alternatively, wipe it out with baking soda sprinkled on a damp rag.)

Your Secret Weapon: Baking Soda

Nothing works better than baking soda for many basic household cleaning chores. Really. This remarkable stuff cleans and deodorizes—what else can you use to adjust the pH in your pool, leaven quick breads, and dry-shampoo the dog?

Baking soda, a sodium bicarbonate, is a naturally occurring substance that can be manufactured by passing carbon dioxide through either mined or processed soda ash. Baking soda is a mild alkali that dissolves dirt and grease, and because it is mildly abrasive is can be used to safely scour sinks, tubs, tile, microwaves, plastic containers or toys... even teeth!

You can cook with it—the leavening agents in baking soda increase the surface area of dough or batter, causing it to become light and porous—and it is one of the most effective substances you can use to extinguish grease or electrical fires, which makes it a safety staple in the kitchen.

One of the most useful properties of baking soda is its ability to neutralize odors. How does it work? Baking soda brings both acidic and basic (alkaline) odor molecules into a more neutral, odor-free state. You can use it to neutralize odors from sour milk (a strong acid) or spoiled fish (a strong base). Baking soda is so effective in fighting odors that it is used industrially, for odor control at sewage-treatment plants and around barns and feedlots.

You can even use it as a personal deodorant, brush your teeth with it, or dissolve a little in water and use it as a mouthwash. Swallow a little and it becomes an antacid, neutralizing the acids that cause heartburn and indigestion. Because it is harmless, it is very safe to use around children or pets. You don't have to worry about the baby getting into the baking soda!

You probably already have an opened box sitting in your refrigerator and freezer, absorbing food odors (be sure to use a different box for baking). Here are some other ways to use this remarkable product:

✦ Add 1/2 cup to every load of laundry for cleaner, fresher clothes.

✦ Add 1/4 cup to the bottom of trash cans.

✦ Add 1 cup to the kitty litter box.

✦ Sprinkle on carpet before vacuuming to absorb odors.

✦ Sprinkle in the dishwasher between uses to keep the inside smelling fresh.

✦ To keep the kitchen sink smelling sweet, pour 1 cup baking soda down the drain followed by 1 cup of vinegar. Allow the bubbling mixture to sit for 10 minutes. Flush with boiling water or hot, running water for 2–3 minutes.

✦ Make a paste with water or lemon juice and allow it to sit on wooden cutting boards for 5–10 minutes.

✦ To freshen a travel mug, fill it with hot water then add a table-spoon of baking soda, then let it sit in the sink overnight. The baking soda solution will remove stale coffee odors and stains.

✦ Use a paste of lemon juice and baking soda to brighten copper pans.

✦ Add a squeeze of lemon and 1/2 cup baking soda to simmering water on the stove to help absorb cooking odors.

✦ Sprinkle 1/2 cup in the bottom of the diaper pail in baby's room.

✦ Fill ashtrays at home or in the car with baking soda to neutralize odors and help extinguish cigars or cigarettes.

✦ Sprinkle in the bottom of shoes or sneakers to counter that "locker room" smell.

✦ Add to swimming pool water to keep it sparkling clear and reduce eye irritation (directions for swimming pool use can be found on the 4-pound box). (See Chapter 11 for more on swimming pools.)

✦ Put an open box in smelly toolboxes, tackle boxes, or other enclosed spaces where odors tend to linger.

✦ Add 1 cup to a pail of hot water and use as a diaper soak to remove ammonia odors.

✦ Flush 1 cup down the toilet periodically to help keep pH levels stable in septic tanks. (This provides a healthy environment for the beneficial bacteria that help break down waste.)

✦ Keep a 4-pound box in the trunk of your car. Nestle the box inside a larger box, such as a shoe box, and poke holes in the box of baking soda, which will allow it to absorb odors more efficiently without spillage. The baking soda also serves as an emergency fire extinguisher.

Lemon Aid

Lemons are another vital natural ingredient for keeping things clean and fresh. Along with the lemon-juice-and-soda tips above, here are some creative ways you can use these self-contained cleaning wonders:

✦ Slice a lemon peel into hunks and feed it down the disposal to make the whole kitchen smell lemony fresh.

✦ Dip the cut end of a lemon in baking soda and use it to shine copper pots.

✦ Rub a cut lemon over (rinsed) wooden cutting boards to absorb odors and neutralize flavors.

✦ Cut up a lemon and add to simmering water on the stove for an instant air freshener.

✦ Rub a lemon slice over your fingers and hands after chopping garlic or onions, to remove the smell.

✦ Keep lemons in a decorative bowl in the kitchen; the display is fresh and inviting, and you'll be more likely to use the lemons if you can see them.

Extend the Life of Fresh Produce

If you've ever come home from the grocery store and tossed a plastic bag of fresh lettuce or cilantro into the crisper of your refrigerator, only to discover three days later that the bag contents have morphed into an unrecognizable mass of green slime, then try these fresh-produce tricks:

✦ Prepare fresh produce for storage as soon as you get home from the store. The sooner you tend to these products, the longer they will last.

✦ Dunk heads of lettuce into a bowl of cold water to which you have added 1 tablespoon of vinegar and 1 tablespoon of sugar. The vinegar will clean any dirt or chemical residue off of the greens, and the sugar will invigorate and crisp the greens. Swish the lettuce around, drain, then loosely wrap in a shroud of paper towels for storage.

✦ Fresh cilantro, or Italian parsley, makes a wonderful accompaniment to many foods, but it turns to slime quickly if it's not adequately prepared for storage. Fortunately, this is an easy task. You can even keep the rubber band around the base of the bundle. Simply rinse the cilantro under cold running water, chop an inch or so off the bottom stalks, then stand the whole bundle upright in a container of water, like a bunch of flowers. Store in the refrigerator. Change the water every two days. Cilantro or curly parsley stored this way can stay fresh for over a week. To use, take the bundle out and slice off the desired amount right off the top, like you're giving the bundle a haircut.

✦ Store celery and asparagus the same way: rinse, slice off the bottoms, then store upright in the refrigerator in a container of fresh water.

Clean-Out-the-Refrigerator Recipes

Keep a few "clean it out" recipes on hand for those times when you find yourself overwhelmed by a crowded pantry or a refrigerator full of fruits and vegetables that are threatening to go bad. If you know in advance what your standby recipes are, then you can keep the basic ingredients on hand.

Here are a few of my favorites:

FILL-'ER-UP FRUIT TART

Filling:
> 2 cups vanilla-flavored yogurt
> 3 eggs
> 1/2 cup sugar
> 1/2 cup flour
> 1 teaspoon vanilla
> 1 teaspoon almond extract

1 frozen pie shell, thawed
All the extra fruit or berries you have on hand (3–4 cups is fine)
Sliced almonds (optional)

Put the pie crust in a deep-dish pie pan. Blend the filling ingredients together until smooth, then pour into the crust. Add all the chopped fruit and berries. Sprinkle with sliced almonds, if desired. Bake at 375 degrees Fahrenheit for 45 minutes, or until brown and bubbly.

This is a great way to use up extra blueberries, blackberries, peaches, strawberries, cherries, even apples. This is not a great way to make use of overripe bananas, however. Pull out a trusted banana bread recipe for those!

POTATO SOUP

> potatoes
> 1/2 a stick of butter
> milk
> salt
> pepper
> onions or scallions

Peel and boil all the extra potatoes you have stashed away that are threatening to sprout. Drain the water, then add half a stick of butter and mash well. Add enough milk to make the soup the desired consistency, then season with salt and pepper. Sauté any extra onions or scallions you have lying around and throw them in.

This soup adapts well to many kinds of creative additions: chicken, turkey, shrimp, bacon, cheese, corn, broccoli, cauliflower—you can toss in just about anything.

QUESADILLAS

> tortillas
> cheese
> diced chicken, beef, shrimp or bacon
> your choice of vegetables

If you always keep grated cheese and tortillas on hand, you can make quesadillas out of just about any other extra ingredients you have available. Diced chicken, beef, shrimp, and bacon all work well. So do most vegetables: grilled or sautéed onions, mushrooms, zucchini or summer squash, tomatoes, red or green bell peppers, and cilantro are all tasty additions.

Place a tortilla in a dry, preheated skillet. Add filling ingredients first, then top with a handful of cheese. Place another tortilla on top. When the underside is brown and crispy, flip it over. The whole thing takes about 10 minutes to prepare, and kids love 'em.

Cool Tips for a Clean Refrigerator

How often has it happened? You move a jug of milk in the refrigerator only to be greeted by a Tupperware container filled with…what? You have no idea. You don't know what it is or how long it's been there. When viewed through the opaque plastic the contents aren't even vaguely recognizable. You'd better clean it out. Oh, this is going to be bad.

Or, you may suffer from a different type of refrigerator mayhem. When you open your refrigerator door you may be greeted by shelves inside that are covered with sticky rings and crusty spills. Jars have dried-on food remnants glazing the sides. Oh, what a mess.

As with other areas of household cleaning, there are a few tricks you should know when it comes to keeping your refrigerator and freezer clean. Here's the biggie:

The secret to keeping your refrigerator clean and sparkly inside is to spot-clean frequently instead of waiting to *Clean Out the Refrigerator*, making it a big production and time-consuming chore. When supplies run low, wipe out a shelf or two. Make refrigerator cleaning an ongoing process.

Clean up spills immediately—don't let them sit. If something does spill, take a hot, wet rag, spritz it with an all-purpose cleanser, then wipe up the spill. If it's a big spill, like an overturned milk jug, soak up the spill with a large, dry towel first. If the spill is minor, wipe it up, then use your wet rag to take a swipe at other areas that look like they could use a little freshening up.

Every day or two, crouch down and take a good look at what's inside. Toss anything that has passed its expiration date, and get rid of any aging leftovers sooner rather than later. Speaking of leftovers, store them in clear glass containers. Opaque containers hide the food, where it tends to be forgotten and then spoil.

Another preventive-maintenance tip: use a warm, damp, clean kitchen towel to wipe off condiment jars and bottles before you put the lid back on and put them back in the refrigerator. Items such as mustard, mayonnaise, and salsa store much cleaner and neater this way.

Use masking tape and a permanent marker to write the date on any items you store in the freezer. Unless you are storing meats in a subzero freezer, make it a habit to use frozen meat, seafood, and poulty within three to six months.

The Perfect Pantry

It is all-too-easy for food storage areas to become crowded with old, forgotten dry staples and packaged foods that are hovering perilously near their expiration date. To avoid stale or forgotten foods, keep your shelves clean, and keep your pantry inventory useful and up-to-date, make it a practice to cull through your pantry shelves once a week and pull out two or three items you can work into your menu during the week. Look for ways to use a forgotten box of risotto, a can of green beans, or a bag of whole wheat pasta you've been meaning to cook for months. Packaged sauces, gravy mixes, and anything in a powdered state such as flour or cornmeal should go on your list of things to use sooner rather than later.

Now, let's get this pantry organized. Begin by grouping like items with like. Put canned goods on one shelf, arrange bags or boxes of pasta together, and place baking ingredients such as baking powder, baking soda, flour, and sugar (always off the floor) in a designated spot. Outwit critters in the pantry by storing flour and sugar in airtight jars or decorative containers. Line boxes of cereal together like soldiers. Some people find that color-coding the contents of their pantry helps keep things in order: yellow canned foods go together, then red, then green, you get the picture.

Look for ways to consolidate items in your pantry. Got two half-eaten boxes of cereal? Seal the inner plastic liners and put both bags in one box. (If you share your cereal with others you may want to put a sticky note on the box, label the liners, or just tell them about the newly devised cereal cohabitation arrangement.) This frees up valuable storage space in the pantry—always a good thing. If you have the space, store backup supplies of grains, flour, nuts, and coffee beans in the freezer, which keeps them fresh and also helps to minimize clutter in the pantry.

Finally, strive to keep floor space clear, which will make it much easier to sweep and mop and keep hungry bugs at bay.

CHOOSE LOW-MAINTENANCE APPLIANCES

✦ Buy major appliances with an eye toward maintaining them and keeping them clean. For example, the easiest refrigerators to clean also tend to be the least expensive—those that have wire shelves. Large planes of plexiglass catch every drip and crumb and get icky fast. (One benefit of glass shelves, however, is that they contain the mess if something liquid spills.)

✦ Do your research. Spend an hour or two in the library or online. Consult *Consumer Reports* to get an idea of which brands and models not only look good, but perform well, too.

✦ Keep in mind that appliances such as dishwashers and refrigerators are energy hogs. If you are in the market for a new appliance, look for one that is energy-efficient.

✦ If your freezer isn't full, add a sack or two of ice, which will help the unit stay cold while consuming less energy.

✦ Things get lost and go bad in massive refrigerators; unless you have a large family, opt for a smaller, more efficient model.

✦ Keep in mind that the more buttons and knobs an appliance has, the more nooks and crannies will need to be cleaned. Opt for the streamlined, clean model every time.

✦ Forgo refrigerators with ice and water dispensers on the front door. These dispensers tend to malfunction and break, and more often than not they spew ice and water all over the floor instead of into a cup.

✦ If you are in the market for a new cooktop, consider a smooth-surface model instead of traditional burners. The smooth surface is *much* easier to clean.

Chapter Four

HOW TO KEEP BATHROOMS
SHINY AND CLEAN

I once had a college roommate who had a remarkable faith in the promises she heard in all types of ads. Her faith extended to ads for cleaning products, too. One day, when our apartment was beginning to become intolerably dirty, we set about to give our tiny abode a thorough, deep cleaning. She took the bathroom.

Later that evening, I pulled the shower curtain aside to take a bath and gazed in wonder at the gloppy, streaked mess in the bathtub. "Hey,

I thought you were going to clean the bathtub," I hollered. "I did!" she hollered back. "I sprayed on the foam cleanser and let the 'Scrubbing Bubbles' do all the work!"

Ah, if only cleaning a bathroom were so easy! Actually, I know now that cleaning the tub doesn't have to be much more difficult than my old roommate's unorthodox (but highly ineffective) approach. The trick lies in an initial, thorough cleaning, then in preventive maintenance. But we'll get to that in a bit.

Bathroom Clutter Busters

First, let's look at the main problem that tends to plague most bathrooms: clutter.

Like the kitchen, bathrooms tend to accumulate a wide and varied assortment of products. Bottles and canisters and vials of cosmetics, deodorant, hair care products, items for the bath, powders, medicines, shaving items, soaps, towels, cotton balls, Q-Tips…is there any end to the number and variety of items that want to take up residence on your bathroom counter?

Over the years I have discovered a method for dealing with these wayward bottles of stuff. It's not an instant fix, but it does gradually solve the problem. Here it is:

Don't buy a single product until the comparable
product you have at home is gone.

If you have four bottles/cans/tins/tubes of hair gel/mousse/spray/pomade, don't even think of purchasing another until all four have been used up and the containers have been thrown away. If you have two deodorants, use them both before you buy another. Three bottles of shampoo? You know the drill.

In the meantime, you need to find a happy home for all these wayward products. A nice, open, plastic container can keep your toiletries contained, yet visible. When you are able to see the products you have, you are more likely to use them.

CULL WHAT YOU HAVE

Combine half-filled bottles of similar products such as shampoo, hand lotion, or liquid hand soap. This is a quick way to reduce bathroom clutter, and in many instances the product you end up with works just as well if not better than the individual products you combined.

What about the products you never use?

If you're like most, a quick inventory of the products in your bathroom yields surprising results. Toiletries tend to be tempting impulse buys at the store, and the result can be a plethora of products that seemed like good purchases at the time. Will you really use a three-year-old container of Egyptian facial mud, dried-up nail polish, makeup remnants from high school, or perfumed lotion that makes you sneeze? It seems wasteful to throw away perfectly useful items, but in these instances the items really are not useful, so you need feel no guilt in tossing them and freeing up valuable space on your bathroom shelves and counters.

TIP: *Give It Away!*

Because toiletries tend to be such easy impulse buys, many of us have items that we really have no use for but that might be very useful for someone else. As you cull through the items in your bathroom, set aside a box for fresh, unopened or opened-once toiletry items that you can drop off at a local women's shelter, where the items will be used and appreciated.

ADOPT SIGNATURE PRODUCTS

When you find a certain product that you love, adopt it and make it your own.

Perfume is probably the toiletry item that is best suited for personalization. If you buy a fragrance every time you run across one you like, your bureau or bathroom counter will soon be littered with expensive bottles and vials. Clutter.

Instead of allowing a myriad of scents to dominate your space, pick your favorite and make it your own. People will come to identify you by your scent. My wonderful Aunt Lynda has worn the same fragrance for years—Shalimar—and I think of her every time I encounter someone wearing it.

Brand loyalty can extend to other types of products, as well. The beauty of finding a product you like and then sticking with it is that you will no longer buy new products, be disappointed with the way they work, and then stash them under the sink where they may be eternally forgotten.

STORE LIKE ITEMS WITH LIKE

To keep things organized and easy to find, store similar items together. Small organizing containers can help. For example, keep all hair-care products in one container, all over-the-counter medicines in another. Have a separate container for nail-care items such as polish remover, tools, and polishes. Use a separate container for sunscreen and after-sun products. Once products are organized like this, you'll never again wander from bathroom closet to bathroom closet looking for fingernail polish or antacids. An added bonus: this system makes it easy to quickly move medicines out of the reach of children.

For makeup, store related items in zip-lock baggies. Lipsticks go in one bag, eye pencils in another, eye shadows in another. You can store all the zip-lock bags together in a drawer, but finding a specific product will be easy since the bags are organized and you can see through the plastic for the item you need.

Keep an Eye on Bathroom Hot Spots

Like any other room in the house, bathrooms usually have two or three places that tend to collect clutter. Flat surfaces are usually to blame. Places such as ledges in the shower, the backs of toilets, and tub and vanity countertops just naturally seem to attract toiletries and accessories. The trick to keeping these items at bay is to have a designated spot for them all. For example, a shower caddy, with room for all your shower accoutrements, can keep bottles of shampoo and conditioner nice and tidy.

While we're finding a spot for all these bathroom necessities, remember to avoid lining things up in rows. This has the effect of visually enlarging the clutter. A small cluster of related items is better than a long row of items spaced out along the length of the countertop or windowsill.

In my bathroom the hot spot is invariably the space around the bathtub, where I tend to accumulate an impressive collection of bath salts, bubbles, oils, and soaps. I love these products, but they do tend to take up a lot of room. The solution? I put it all in a decorative basket, and I *use the products* every time I take a bath. I take great delight in using the last little bit of a product and throwing the bottle away, getting rid of it, freeing up space in my basket. As soon as my collection is whittled down, the holidays roll around or I have a birthday and the basket gets filled back up, but that's okay, because I know the collection is manageable.

Every so often I run across a product I'm not so wild about—maybe it was a gift or an impulse buy, but if I find that I have a product I don't love, I give it away (see box on page 75). Why keep a product I don't like and am not likely to use, when someone else may enjoy it? I put it in my box of items to give away and don't give it a second thought.

Another common bathroom hot spot is the sink counter.

Lots of people keep their sink counters beautifully accessorized with lovely towels and soaps and an occasional candle or flower arrangement, and they look like something you'd find in a model or sample home, but there isn't a single product in sight that will actually be used. Problems arise when the *useful items* vie for space with the *accessories*. There usually isn't room for both, and even if there is, the useful stuff generally isn't all that attractive to look at.

The key is to figure out what you want to look at, then put the rest of it away, out of sight. Here's how:

Using Space Wisely

In many bathrooms space is at a premium. Take a step back and look at the available storage space in your bathroom objectively. In many cases you can modify your storage methods and free up extra space.

For example, towels and folded sheets take up lots of valuable storage space in many bathrooms, but there may be a way around these storage-space hogs. Here are a few ideas:

✦ Rather than storing fresh towels folded, roll them and place them in decorative baskets beside the shower or tub.

✦ Install large, strong hooks on the bathroom wall, within reach of the shower or tub, where towels can be stored and can also hang to dry once they've been used. Be sure to allow room for air to circulate around the drying towels, to prevent mildew from gaining a foothold. If possible, install the hooks on the wall over AC/heating vents, where the circulating air will help them dry quickly.

✦ If wall space is at a premium, install hooks for towels behind the bathroom door. (These hooks are also useful for storing bathrobes.)

✦ If you have a generous amount of space around the bathtub, a fluffy stack of towels can be tied with a decorative ribbon and "stored" there as a practical accessory.

✦ Invest in a hotel-style, heavy-duty towel rack that can be installed in the space above the toilet. These elegant fixtures add a considerable amount of space in even tiny bathrooms—it's the equivalent of an extra shelf.

✦ Turn a milk crate on its side under the sink; store folded towels inside the milk crate, then set a basket of toiletry items on top.

✦ Many of us keep far more towels on hand than we need or actually use. Store three or four towels in the bathroom, then stash the rest in another part of the house, where storage space is at less of a premium.

✦ Once you get rid of extra, unused toiletries from around the house, you may discover extra storage space in a guest room bath, for example. Store unused towels there and free up space where you really need it (in the master bath).

✦ To keep your towels looking newer longer, purchase towels in a color that is dark enough that it will help hide stains, but light enough to not fade drastically after many washings. Colors such as tan, peach, and sage green wear well, while black and white, for example, either show stains too readily or fade too quickly with repeated washing.

✦ Don't succumb to the temptation to buy decorative towels that can't be washed without destroying the fancy trim. Instead, buy high-quality, color-coordinated towels that can actually be used.

✦ When you buy new towels, donate the old ones to charity or relegate them to the laundry room, where they can be used for cleaning or washing cars. Don't allow them to share space with the new towels!

Bed linens—sheets, blankets, comforters, or bedspreads—are also storage hogs. Rather than store them in the bathroom where you are already challenged for space, store them in or around the area where they will actually be used—the bedroom (see Chapter 5).

More Storage Solutions

✦ If bathroom storage space is tight, take advantage of nearby closets to help deal with overflow. A tower of floor-to-ceiling shelves installed in a nearby closet can take the pressure off crowded shelves and cabinets in the bathroom.

✦ If storage space is really scarce, consider using a piece of furniture in the bathroom, such as a wicker etegère.

✦ Buy multipurpose items. Instead of having a bottle of shampoo and a bottle of conditioner, buy a 2-in-1 product. You'll save time *and* valuable storage space. Do you really need hair gel, mousse, and spray? Try to get by with fewer products.

✦ Hang appliances like your hair dryer or electric shaver from a space-saving wall hook. Makeup and/or shaving mirrors on swing-arm hinges can also be attached to the wall, to further reduce countertop clutter.

✦ Hang a clear plastic shoe-storage hanger on the back of the bathroom door, where it can store toiletry items such as hair spray, brushes, shaving cream, and makeup.

✦ Pull-out shelves or rotating storage carousels under the sink can make items stored there easier to both see and reach.

✦ Use a compartmentalized organizer in a drawer to keep toiletry items organized.

✦ Store seasonal toiletry items such as sunscreen in a less-central space, and remember that sunscreen can lose some of its effectiveness over time. If you don't know exactly how old that tube of orange gelée sunscreen glop is, but it's been around for years, then toss it.

✦ Store extra toilet paper rolls in a decorative, lidded basket near the toilet.

Keeping It Clean

The best way to keep your bathroom sparkling clean is to clean *preventively*—before things get out of control. Teach your family to clean as they go. It's difficult to scrape a week's worth of toothpaste glop out of a sink, but it's easy to quickly swab out the sink after each use with a damp washrag or disinfectant wipe.

Similarly, hard-water stains are very difficult to remove from tile or a shower door, but it's easy to spritz a daily-use shower cleaner such as Clean Shower (or a mild solution of vinegar and water) after using the shower, which will prevent the hard-water buildup from occurring in the first place. These mild cleaners work by keeping shower tile and grout chemically inhospitable to germs and bacteria. Spritz them on after you shower and let the cleaners do the work for you. For glass shower doors, spray the cleaner on, then use a squeegee to swipe the doors clean. The trickling residue will work its way into cracks and crevices and help keep those surfaces clean, too.

Keeping the toilet area clean is now a breeze thanks to the advent of pop-up quick wipes, but you don't have to rely on expensive wipes to keep things sparkly clean. A damp rag or paper towel spritzed with all-purpose cleanser works just as well. Give the porcelain a quick swipe when you first notice that things are looking anything less than pristine.

Another great bathroom shortcut is to keep a toilet brush soaking in all-purpose disinfecting cleanser in an enclosed toilet-brush caddy. You'll have a disinfected brush ready to effortlessly swish the toilet bowl every day.

Preventive cleaning, or spot cleaning, or cleaning only on an as-needed basis in the bathroom will go a long way toward buying time between the hard cleanings. In fact, if you do it right, you'll never have to spend an hour cleaning the bathroom again.

DOUBLE DUTY

Take advantage of opportunities to clean the bathroom as they arise. As you make use of the bathroom, prime opportunities to clean will present themselves.

- ✦ If you have young children, you can clean the kids' bathroom while you supervise them taking a bath, for example. You're already in the bathroom; use the time productively.

- ✦ Clear off and straighten the counter while you brush your teeth. Afterwards, check the faucet and mirror for splats and splatters, then wipe off any offending spots with a slightly damp washrag.

- ✦ After taking a shower or a bath, if your towel has been used a few times and is going into the laundry basket anyway, use it to quick-mop the floor.

- ✦ Toward the end of your bath, let a few inches of water drain out, then use a wrung-out washrag to wipe off the ring around the tub.

- ✦ Spritz the mirror with glass cleaner and wipe it down while you brush your teeth.

- ✦ If you have to let the water run for a couple of minutes for hot water to arrive in your shower, use the time to quickly cull through closets and remove extra wire hangers and straighten shoes. The appearance of most closets can be dramatically improved with just two minutes' worth of attention!

Lots of opportunities like these will present themselves if you keep your eyes open and look for them.

QUICK 5: CLEANING BATHROOMS IN A PINCH

What's this? Company is on the way and you don't have time to clean the bathroom? Use this five-minute, five-step approach:

1. Clear off the countertop. Put bottles, sprays, deodorants, and other toiletry items under the sink or in a decorative container.

2. Wipe down all surfaces with a disposable quick-wipe or damp rag.

3. Throw used towels in a hamper and replace with fresh, clean hand towels.

4. Splash a heavy-duty cleanser in the toilet, to deodorize the entire room. Wipe off the toilet with a disposable towelette or a rag dampened with cleanser.

5. Empty the waste basket.

TIP: *Banish Sponges Forever from Bathroom Duty*

Sponges have a unique ability to harbor and then breed bacteria. The *last place on earth* you ever want to see or use a sponge is in the bathroom. Use disposable quick wipes or old washcloths or kitchen towels that can easily be laundered after every use instead.

Products to Make Your Bathroom Sparkle

In many cases the generic forms of brand-name products work every bit as well as their pricier counterparts, but there are a few unique products that work particularly well. Here they are, broken down by category:

Abrasive cleanser—Barkeeper's Friend. A little bit sprinkled on a damp rag will wipe the scum right out of any sink, tub, or shower stall. Particularly useful for removing globs of toothpaste in the sink, or stubborn rings around the bathtub. (Be careful to only use abrasive cleansers on surfaces that won't scratch.)

Non-abrasive cleanser—There are several effective nonabrasive cleansers on the market, such as Soft Scrub; just be sure you use them with an equally non-abrasive applicator, such as a washcloth or soft cleaning rag. These products work great for cleaning fiberglass and acrylic surfaces.

All-purpose cleanser—409 or Pine-Sol. My favorites.

All-purpose disinfectant—Mr. Clean. Nothing beats it. The strong chemical smell is too much for some, although others (like me) love the unmistakable scent that indicates that things are clean clean clean.

Glass cleaner—Windex. Try replacing it with a generic version. You'll see why the name-brand version is better.

Toilet bowl cleaner—Lysol Cling. The ingenious design allows you to squirt cleaner into the areas that need it the most, while the thick, viscous formula keeps the stain-busting antibacterial agents around to work for a while, making this product the hands-down favorite.

TIP: *Rescue for Rust*

If you find yourself faced with the prospect of cleaning a truly icky, rust-stained, disgustingly neglected, foul toilet, cast your regular cleaning products aside and get serious. Head down to your local hardware store for some sodium bisulfate. Sprinkle in 1/4 cup and pop on your rubber gloves for a single heavy-duty scrub, then flush. If the rust still refuses to yield, pull out the big guns: wet/dry sandpaper, or extra-fine steel wool.

If you have a consistent problem with rust stains, in the toilet or elsewhere, consider using water-treatment products that can restore proper alkalinity to the water and solve the problem at its source. (www.Rust Solver.com is a good source of products designed to remove rust.)

A NATURAL CLEAN

I love the nice, lemony, sanitized smell that only Pine-Sol can provide, but there are those who prefer a more natural approach. The good news is that many inexpensive, common household products can be used to make your house sparkle.

The main products you will need are vinegar, baking soda, and household ammonia. Vinegar is naturally acidic and can be used to cut through grime and grease. It's great for removing bathtub rings and scum in the shower. Baking soda is mildly abrasive and is very effective in loosening and scouring bathtub surfaces. Ammonia is a highly concentrated but toxic cleaner; keep it out of the reach of pets or children. For general use in the bathroom, add 1/2 cup of ammonia to 1 gallon of hot water (be sure to wear rubber gloves when you clean with ammonia).

Let These Products Do the Heavy Lifting

Unfortunately, bathrooms suffer from an ongoing onslaught of dirt and germs. As soon as they've been cleaned, the onslaught resumes. But there are a few products out there that keep working to keep the bathroom clean even when you're not actively scrubbing. You don't even have to be in the room.

Biological drain treatments are designed to keep pipes cleaner and clearer by introducing bacteria that feed on organic matter in those accumulations—a much safer alternative to chemical cleaners.

These treatments use enzymes to stage an initial hit-and-run attack on organic matter in the pipe. The real working agents in these treatments come from microorganisms that break down and digest organic material. The microorganisms eventually flourish in pipes to provide a continuous, live-in cleanup crew.

Microorganisms will not eat everything; things like hair are indigestible. But bacteria eat away at sticky organic stuff that often binds hair and other material together, or that holds it to pipes, so the hair can be effectively flushed from the pipe.

There are several benefits from using biological treatments: they don't harm pipes because there are no harmful corrosive agents, they are safe around children and pets, they don't harm the environment, and they clean continuously. The downside is that they can take a while to work; most begin working after an overnight application, then additional product needs to be added occasionally until the bacterial colony is fully established. You can buy these products online; check out www.PlumbingStore.com.

Toilet bowl disinfectant tablets are another product that can dramatically reduce the amount of time you spend cleaning your bathroom. These disinfecting tablets clean continuously while you're off doing something more enjoyable. (A word of warning: only use disinfecting chemical tablets in toilets that are flushed at least once a day. The chemicals can become corrosive if left in an unused toilet too long.)

Tips for Bathroom Maintenance

✦ Keep a generously sized waste basket in the bathroom. This is a room that tends to generate a lot of trash, and the last thing you need in your otherwise-clean bathroom is an overflowing waste basket.

✦ Store cleaning products for the bathroom in a bucket that you keep *in the bathroom*. Keep the bucket beneath a counter or tucked inside a linen closet. You want to keep your cleaning supplies within easy reach, so that quick spot-cleaning becomes effortless.

+ If you keep a drinking glass in the bathroom, make sure it is white enamel or plastic, not clear or dark glass or plastic. Clear or dark materials highlight toothpaste residue and look disgusting in no time.

+ Don't throw away that old toothbrush just yet! Before you toss it, spritz it with your favorite bathroom cleaner and quickly clean the nooks and crannies around the sink and faucet, where grime tends to accumulate. Wipe the area clean with a damp rag. *Now* you can throw the old toothbrush away!

+ If you keep reading materials in the bathroom, keep the supply current and whittled down. Keep the supply contained; a basket works well. Every time you put a new magazine in the bathroom, pull one from the basket and toss it into the recycling bin.

+ Watch out for newspapers in the bathroom—they can clutter the space very quickly. Cull them every day.

+ Use area rugs or floor mats to protect solid floors and carpeted surfaces from hair spray, makeup, and other personal-care products.

+ Rubbing alcohol will quickly and completely remove a glaze of hair spray from mirrors.

+ To quickly clean a shower head without taking the whole thing apart, fill a sturdy plastic bag with vinegar and use a rubber band to hold it on the shower head overnight.

+ Lemon oil furniture polish will remove water spots on metal frames around shower doors.

+ Keep knickknacks and accessories to a minimum, since they are magnets for dust, powder, and overspray from hair-care products.

✦ *Never* fold a still-damp towel. Hang it on a sturdy wall hook to dry, or drape it over a towel rod. Make sure lots of fresh air can circulate around the drying towel, to prevent the growth of mildew.

✦ If you have a shower curtain, line it with a mildew-resistant liner. If your shower curtain liner is streaked with mold, mildew, and soap scum, try this trick: toss it in the washing machine with two towels. Add 1/2 cup of detergent and 1/2 cup of baking soda. Add a cup of vinegar to the rinse cycle, then hang the curtain to let it drip-dry, or toss it in the dryer with the towels for up to five minutes. If the liner has become brittle, add a few drops of mineral oil to a damp washcloth and toss it in the dryer with the liner, or add a few drops of oil to the final rinse water.

✦ Denture-cleaning tablets do a great job of cleaning toilets. Drop in several tablets, let them foam, leave the solution in the toilet for 10–15 minutes, then scrub and flush.

✦ Cola that has gone flat can also be used to clean porcelain toilets. Pour the cola in, let it soak for an hour, then flush.

✦ Before leaving town, pour a splash of all-purpose cleanser into toilets, to prevent hard-water rings from forming.

✦ To remove a fine film of hair spray from bathroom counters, clear everything off the counter, then spray the surface liberally with an all-purpose cleanser. Let the cleaner sit on the gunk for five minutes, then wipe off with a warm, damp rag.

✦ If hair tends to accumulate on your bathroom floor, suck it up with the nozzle attachment of a vacuum cleaner. If the floor area is small, you can use a wet paper towel to capture the loose hairs.

✦ Try to avoid wallpaper in bathrooms. The steam can loosen the paper and mildew can grow between the paper and the wall. Worse, if there's ever a leak behind the wall, the wallpaper can mask the damage until the problem is out of control. A high-quality semigloss paint is a better choice.

✦ Some soaps leave a harder residue than others. Hard-milled soaps tend to be the worst offenders, while the residue left behind by more gentle varieties such as Dove or Ivory are easier to remove. Liquid soaps leave the least amount of residue.

✦ A bar of soap that is too small to use effectively can be pressed into the sides of a new bar softened by recent use.

✦ Use specially formulated disposable towelettes or a dark-colored washcloth for removing makeup; your light-colored washcloths will last longer if you don't use them for makeup removal.

TIP: *Keep Things Smelling Sweet*

It's an unfortunate but undeniable fact: bathrooms sometimes don't smell good. An all-natural citrus air freshener can remove even stubborn smells: use an orange- or lemon-based freshener that will eliminate odors, not just mask them. (Citrus-based air fresheners are also great for eliminating cooking odors in the kitchen or keeping the baby's room smelling fresh and sweet.)

Carmen, the Bathroom Master

Before you reach the point where you can keep your bathroom sparkly with just basic maintenance, a good, thorough cleaning may first be in order.

I once had a housekeeper, Carmen, who made my bathrooms sparkle like new. "What's your secret, Carmen?" I asked her one day, shaking my head in wonder. "You've got to use lots of elbow grease," she replied, "and you can't be afraid of getting wet!"

I watched her work. She popped on her yellow rubber gloves and got to work. She stepped into the shower, then worked up a good Mr.

Clean lather, scrubbing the shower door and walls with a wet, sudsy washrag in small, circular motions. Once the shower was covered in foam she took a large cup and poured hot water down the walls, and shower door, removing the suds, soap scum and all. Finally she stepped out of the shower and scrubbed the shower floor, this time relying on a gritty cleanser such as Barkeeper's Friend or Comet. When she was done, she used a squeegee to dry the door and walls then wiped the whole thing down with a clean towel spritzed with glass cleaner. Voilà!

She moved to the tub, and my eyes widened as she climbed in and got to work. More scrubbing with small, circular motions, more Mr. Clean, more hot water. Once again, she dried the inside of the tub when she was finished, using the damp towel to polish the chrome fixtures as she dried.

Carmen moved on to the counters. She put things away with startling speed and efficiency. Powder, deodorant, and hair spray were quickly moved beneath the sink; toothpaste and hair accessories went in drawers; perfume and cologne bottles were grouped together and dusted with a quick swish of yet another damp rag. Then she sprayed down the entire surface with an all-purpose cleanser, cleaned the mirrors, then polished the chrome fixtures last. I was breathless.

Next, she attacked the toilet. Lots of Lysol Cling, lots of scrubbing with a toilet brush, then finally she splashed full-strength cleanser onto yet another damp rag and wiped the whole thing down, top to bottom. As she cleaned, Carmen informed me that, because of the different types of stains that tend to plague porcelain—including hard-water stains, which are notoriously difficult to remove—cleaning a badly stained, grimy toilet can require multiple passes with full-strength chemical cleansers, and *lots* of elbow grease.

Carmen finished by pulling all the area rugs, used towels, and a now-impressive stack of used cleaning rags out of the bathroom. She put them all into the washing machine, then washed them all in hot water. She went back to the bathroom and finished by damp-mopping with hot, sudsy water. My bathroom was eat-off-the-floor clean, and I had had a lesson from a pro.

What amazed me the most about this lesson was the fact that it really didn't take that long. Twenty, thirty minutes tops, and she was done. Carmen worked quickly and thoroughly. She didn't stop to grab a snack, call a friend, or watch the morning news. Focusing on the job at hand makes it go much more quickly.

Key lessons from Carmen:

- ✦ Start with the least germy surfaces and work your way toward the most germ-ridden surface in the room (the toilet).

- ✦ Clean the floor last.

- ✦ Use the right product for the job.

- ✦ Don't be afraid of getting wet.

- ✦ Cleaning the bathroom well doesn't have to take all day if you roll up your sleeves and avoid distraction.

- ✦ Put bathroom clutter and personal care products away *before* you start to clean.

Simplify with Easy-Clean Bathroom Décor

After living in eight different houses in twelve years, I came to the realization that some bathroom décor elements are easier to clean and keep clean than others.

For example, while black counters and floors—formica, tile, or granite—are sleek and dramatic, they also highlight every loose hair and smear of toothpaste.If you are considering a move or are in the process of building or remodeling, choose your design elements with easy cleaning and organizing in mind.

Here are a few elements to consider:

- ✦ Gold-tone (brass) fixtures show water spots more readily than their silver-toned (chrome) cousins.

✦ Clear shower glass highlights water spots; frosted glass does not.

✦ Carpeting the bathroom is not a good idea; solid, water-resistant surfaces like tile or marble work better.

✦ Grouted tile surfaces are more difficult to clean and keep clean than smooth surfaces; epoxy grout is easier to clean than traditional grout, and it resists mold and mildew as well. Match dark tile with equally dark grout.

✦ Solid-color surfaces reveal loose hairs, dust, and makeup smudges, while swirly, two-toned patterns help disguise less-than-pristine conditions between cleanings.

✦ Built-in storage looks cleaner and more streamlined than after-the-fact storage containers. If you're building, go ahead and build in lots of shelves, cabinets, and drawers.

✦ Most people store their ironing board and iron in the laundry room, but a small, compact version built into the bathroom wall (if there's space) can save a lot of time and energy for quick touch-ups as you dress.

✦ A dimmer switch can help fill the room with a soothing, warm glow, without having to burn 15 cluttering candles to get the same effect. Use the dimmer switch, and light one or two candles instead.

✦ Place low-wattage nightlights in bathrooms, which eliminates the need to flick on blazing bright lights for middle-of-the-night visits.

✦ Hang a magazine rack on the wall by the toilet to store reading materials.

✦ Make use of space that is often wasted: the wall above the toilet is a great place to hang a cabinet or additional shelving.

Chapter Five

BEDROOM AND LAUNDRY

Ah, the bliss of a well-appointed, restful bedroom, a port in the storm, a haven from the stress of the world that surrounds us....

What's that, you say? Your bedroom isn't well-appointed or restful?

There are four laundry baskets of folded clothes on the floor, stacks of books and magazines, and an ironing board set up in the corner?

Well, cheer up. There are lots of ways to make your bedroom a well-appointed, restful haven. I'm about to show you how.

The Restful Room

It's nice when your kitchen is clean, great when the family room is all picked up, super when the floors are clean. But having a well-appointed, restful bedroom is more than just a *nice-to-have*. In today's society, when we all face pressures and stress, having a relaxing, restful place to go is *vital*. When you make your bed in the morning, pick clothes up off the floor, and straighten books and knickknacks, consider this an investment in your well-being, not just another chore to do around the house.

Get in the habit of taking care of your bedroom before you even leave the room in the morning. Making the bed takes about a minute, but it sends an unmistakable message: today the house isn't going to win. It starts everything off on the right foot.

Appraising Your Décor

Before we delve into keeping this room clean and clutter free, let's back up a bit and consider the basic elements of your bedroom décor. Is the room freshly painted, or are the walls dingy and in need of repair? Is the carpet stained and faded? Is the furniture in need of repair? You may not be able to fix all of these things at once, but take note of the general condition of this room and resolve to get it in shape.

Because bedrooms are semi-private, they all too often become repositories for unwanted pieces of furniture that don't work anywhere else. If you have an odd chair, decrepit desk, or unused exercise equipment junking up your bedroom, sell or give it away. Reclaim your space.

While the bedroom is a great place to surround yourself with reminders of the people and places you love, get rid of any knickknacks that don't have a positive mental association or useful function. Those items are just clutter.

Adequate lighting is a key element in the bedroom. If you like to read in bed, install a swing-arm lamp on the wall beside the bed, which will free up space on the bedside table and makes a better reading light than a lamp on the table anyway. Look for a nightstand that has lots of storage space for books and magazines. Mine has a door on the side so I can keep my stacks of books out of sight. (A friend of mine once let a decorator talk her into a contemporary, all-glass nightstand. As a result, nothing was hidden; all her bedside items, including tissues and lip balm, were on display—all the time. She hated it.)

If you have a CD player *and* an alarm clock crowding the space on your bureau or nightstand, use them somewhere else and find a combination CD player/alarm clock to conserve space and reduce clutter.

Finally, take a step back and examine the elements of your bedroom décor that are not working well or could be improved. For example, if you have a cat with dark fur who likes to sleep on your bed, then you are just asking for trouble if you have a light-colored comforter or duvet on your bed. Find a coverlet that will hide the fur, or, better yet, have your pet sleep on a towel or blanket that can be easily and frequently washed.

Grouping similar items together is another way to improve functionality in the bedroom. If you have a collection of figurines or candles or perfume bottles or clocks or button boxes or whatever, consider a hanging wall display that can keep the pieces together and contained, rather than having the pieces scattered throughout the room. The collection becomes easier to process and enjoy visually when it is contained.

Developing Neat Bedroom Habits

If you want your bedroom to be a soothing and restful port in the storm, you'll need to develop a few, basic good habits to keep it in shape.

First, the no-brainer: make your bed every morning. It takes one minute and makes the room look pulled together for the rest of the day. You're off to a good start!

If making your bed is a pain in the neck, try this trick: at the corners, pin the blanket to the comforter or duvet cover, so you eliminate the hassle of finding, smoothing, and tucking the blanket altogether. This trick works especially well for beds that are against the wall or are in some other way difficult to make (and it works great for children's beds, too).

If you have a hardwood or tile floor in your bedroom, place an area rug by the side of the bed, so you can wipe dirt and dust off your feet and keep it from coming to bed with you.

If your bed is against a wall, make sure you use a headboard, which will keep the wall behind the bed from becoming dinged-up or soiled.

Whenever you change your clothes, put dirty clothes straight into the clothes hamper. Completely eliminate their midway resting spot on the floor, on the back of a chair, on the foot of the bed, or on the ironing board or the arm of the exercise machine in the corner.

Before you leave the room in the morning, train yourself to give it a sweeping glance. You're looking for items to take with you as you leave the room: books or magazines that have already been read, cups or mugs to go back to the kitchen, or clothing to take to the cleaners.

Finally, if you have children, help them pick up their rooms every evening before bed. Do it with them. This isn't heavy-duty cleaning, but rather an exercise in instilling good bedroom habits at a young, impressionable age. Toss toys in the toy basket, put books back on the shelf, put dirty clothes in the hamper, and put clean clothes away. That way the room will be picked up and ready for play the next day, and—an added bonus—you'll be teaching your kids to appreciate an orderly room.

QUICK 5: CLEANING THE BEDROOM IN A PINCH

1. Make the bed.
2. Put all dirty clothes or stray towels in the hamper.
3. Straighten books and magazines.
4. Dust with a damp washrag or disposable wipe.
5. Open curtains or window coverings to let the light stream in.

Clutter-Busting Your Bedroom

Ridding your bedroom of clutter can be a Herculean task. If you've been storing things away in your bedroom, using it as a place to stash IWAH (Items Without a Home), then you'll need to approach this task with a big, empty box and a lot of resolve. You may need to divide the job into manageable tasks and plan to do the job in two or three sessions.

On the first pass through the room, get rid of the obvious, useless clutter: old magazines, unwanted knickknacks, books you have already read. Either throw this stuff away or put it in the box of things you will give to charity. Next, put away all the IWAH. If you want to keep something, find a permanent spot for it, or get rid of it.

Finally, cast a ruthless eye on the *flat surfaces* in the room: dresser tops, nightstands, and bureau tops are all prime resting spots for clutter. If you have an obvious hot spot, see if it can be done away with entirely. I once had a large cedar chest in my bedroom that somehow ended up being the final resting place for a large, wide variety of IWAH. Because of the vast and varied collection on the top of the cedar chest, the room always looked cluttered. Once I moved the cedar chest to another room, my bedroom miraculously shed the tendency it had to attract clutter.

TYPICAL BEDROOM HOT SPOTS

Here are a few tips for conquering typical bedroom hot spots:

✦ Exercise equipment in the bedroom is a magnet for worn clothing that somehow just can't make it all the way to the closet. If you have a treadmill, elliptical trainer, weight bench, or other type of exercise equipment in your bedroom and it is *not* doing double-duty as a mid-room valet, pat yourself on the back and skip to the next bullet. But if your exercise equipment attracts miscellaneous items of clothing like a second-hand store, it's time to find another spot to keep the equipment. Try the garage,

an extra bedroom, or even a corner of the living room, where a
well-placed screen can ensure its virtual invisibility.

✦   Use a dresser tray to collect jewelry you wear on a daily basis,
    pocket change, and anything else you pull from your pockets at
    the end of the day, and keep a waste basket nearby, so wadded
    tissues, ticket stubs, useless business cards, and chewing gum
    wrappers can go straight into the trash without languishing on
    your dresser top first.

✦   Get knickknacks off the flat surfaces. A well-placed curio cabi-
    net can showcase your treasures and keep them clean and dust-
    free, too.

✦   For maximal impact, group photos together in similar types of
    frames—silver, wood, whatever. A hodgepodge collection of
    photos in various types of frames looks cluttered, but housing
    the same photos in similar frames draws the viewer's eye to the
    photos themselves, instead of the varied collection of frames.

✦   For very small bedrooms, take advantage of every bit of avail-
    able space by installing hooks behind doors, where bulky
    bedroom items such as robes can be easily and unobtrusively
    stored.

✦   Dolls and stuffed animals on a bed can be charming, but finding
    a place for all of them once you're ready to actually use the bed
    can be a challenge. One way to solve this problem is to install a
    wall shelf over the bed; the dolls and stuffed animals can still
    preside over the bedroom, but they don't have to be taken off
    the bed at night or rearranged in the morning.

✦   If you like to nosh in the bedroom, keep a small tray handy so
    empty cups and plates can easily be returned to the kitchen.
    And choose the foods you eat in the bedroom carefully: avoid
    anything crispy or crunchy, which will leave a trail of crumbs.
    Opt for simple fruits, cheese, or bite-sized snacks instead.

- ✦ If you drink coffee or tea in bed in the mornings, then you understand that an occasional drip or spill is inevitable. Choose bed linens accordingly.

- ✦ If you share your bedroom with pets, keep a small hand vacuum under the bed so you can quickly and easily remove clumps of fur or specks of dirt that the pets leave behind.

Dust-Busting Your Bedroom

Keep a container of dusting wipes, such as Old English Furniture Wipes, in an inconspicuous place in your bedroom, so you can whip out a wipe and remove dust in a matter of seconds.

For trouble spots, such as lampshades, use a hair dryer to gently blow the dust off, then let the dust settle for a few minutes before using the furniture wipes to clean the blown dust off the furniture nearby (always blow the dust off in the direction of easy-to-clean furniture, not the bed!). If you don't have a hair dryer, a feather duster or vacuum brush attachment will work, too.

Bedrooms that are dark tend to accumulate dust more than their lighter counterparts simply because the dust is more difficult to see, so the need to dust is often overlooked. If your bedroom tends to be dark, make it a point to grab a quick wipe and dust now and then, whether or not you see an obvious layer of dust.

Many bedrooms have ceiling fans, which help circulate air and provide a nice breeze on warm summer nights, and redistribute warm air in the winter. The downside, however, is that ceiling fans sit there all year long, collecting dust that floats through the air. Because the tops of the blades are out of sight, they are often overlooked as a spot that needs to be cleaned.

To keep your ceiling fan from becoming a whirling distributor of dust, wipe the tops of the blades with a damp rag every two or three months, or use a feather duster frequently, to keep the dust at bay.

> ## *Quick-Clean Supplies to Keep in the Bedroom*
>
> ✓ Old English Furniture Wipes or Swiffer cloths, for dusting furniture and knickknacks.
> ✓ Unger Total Reach-Plus Duster ($30) for reaching cobwebs, behind the bed, and other hard-to-reach places (800-833-6100).
> ✓ Windex Glass and Surface Wipes, for cleaning mirrors, windows, and switchplates in a pinch.

What Do We Have Here, Under the Bed?

When I first saw the film *No Way Out* with Kevin Costner, I knew the dead woman was not to be pitied the moment someone looked under her bed and found nothing but an old Polaroid film negative. Yeah, right. *Nothing under her bed.* I just couldn't relate.

Only the most disciplined, austere souls have the ability to shun the space beneath their beds as a last-minute refuge of sorts for all kinds of bedroom debris. By using this space wisely, however, you can thwart the evil forces that would have you shove dirty clothes, mismatched shoes, mateless socks, and an occasional soda can into this most tempting of space vacuums.

To use this space wisely, it helps a great deal to spend a few bucks on storage containers designed specifically to be used under beds. They're slim, compact, and covered, and many of them are on wheels. What to put in them? This is a great spot to store extra blankets and sheets for the bed, wrapping paper, and out-of-season clothes.

Use an under-the-bed plastic storage box to store clean sheets. Put a dryer sheet in the box or a perfumed sachet to keep the linens smelling sweet. Stash a box under each bed, so you'll never have to wonder where the sheets are for a particular bed or riffle through stacks of sheets in the linen closet searching for the right sheets.

The beauty of using real storage solutions under the bed is that not only do you gain functional storage there, but you prevent the space from becoming a hungry, sucking void that fills on its own accord with random bits of bedroom debris. You can find a wide and varied selection of under-bed storage solutions at www.ContainerStore.com or www.HoldEverything.com.

Sickrooms and Messy Patients

Outwitting the mess that a sickroom entails requires a bit of determination and focus. In many cases a sick person makes a lot of messes— some of which they have absolutely no control over, and others that are simply a by-product of being stuck in a room and not feeling well. A person with a stomach flu will understandably need to hurl once in a while; a patient with a raging head cold is bound to leave a trail of tissues in his wake.

You can deal with both types of disarray by planning ahead.

Don't count on a patient who is throwing up—especially a child— to be able to make it to the toilet before the eruption occurs. Give them a container with a handle—Tupperware works great—so they won't have to make a mad dash for the bathroom when their stomach turns. For a really sick patient, cover the bed with a washable blanket, so any wayward yucky substances can be easily cleaned up.

The other type of mess that a sick patient usually makes is the more garden-variety type: piles of books and magazines, used cups and plates, tissue boxes and medicine containers and the *TV Guide* and remote control and…and everything they could possibly need, all within reach.

Keeping the accoutrements of an illness contained takes a bit of forethought, but it can be done.

First, put a waste basket *with a liner* within easy reach of the patient. Put the objects that tend to generate a lot of trash—such as boxes of tissue—near the container.

To keep the area around the patient from being overwhelmed by used plates and eating utensils, serve them on sturdy but disposable dinnerware. The patient can eat and then clean up the mess in one effortless toss into the trash container.

To avoid a collection of drinking cups, provide the patient with a large, insulated mug with a straw—the kind hospitals use.

Baskets and other types of containers can help keep things organized on a table beside the patient. Use one for books and magazines, another for cards, and another for medicines. If the patient is taking several different types of medication, use a drawer organizer, and use the different compartments for medicines, lip balm, eye drops, and whatever else the patient wants to keep handy.

Finally, take extra care to keep surfaces clean and disinfected. Keep disinfecting hand gel and a container of disposable, disinfecting handiwipes nearby to quickly wipe up spills and to clean germy surfaces frequently.

These measures can help keep the patient comfortable, can make keeping the area clean much easier, and can keep the illness from spreading to other family members and visiting friends.

Closets: Making the Most out of the Space You Have

In our frequent moves, my husband and I have come to appreciate the differences between cramped, crowded closets that tend to quickly fall into a state of disarray, and closets that are outfitted with organized storage in mind. The difference is unbelievable.

Closets that are nothing but big (or small), empty rooms provide no organizational skeleton; there are no storage options. On the other hand, closets that are outfitted with racks and shelves maximize the allotted space and make organization a breeze. If your closets are a mess, chances are they have not been properly outfitted.

Getting a closet maximized for storage does not require spending a bundle on hiring a professional closet organizer. Do-it-yourself stores such as Lowe's or Home Depot have everything you need to bring organization and order to the most disheveled of closets. There are lots of great websites devoted to closet organization, too, including www.ClosetMaid.com, www.EasyClosets.com, and www.SmartFurniture.com.

Before you start installing racks, take a careful inventory of the items you want to store in the closet. Consider your needs first. Do you need ample space for long, hanging garments, such as dresses or coats? Do you need to provide a space to store unused luggage? How many shoes, belts, bags, and purses do you need to store? Get an idea of your needs and sketch out a plan before you go shopping for materials or storage components.

Once the shelves and racks are in place, don't fill them haphazardly with stuff. Group like items with like: sweaters on one shelf, jeans on another. Group out-of-season or seldom-used items together. For the clothes items that are in season, group them together first by article of clothing, then by color: light shirts, dark shirts, light pants, dark pants, you get the picture.

Use a canvas, hanging shoe sorter to keep shoes together and off the floor of the closet, or store shoes in clear plastic shoe boxes. If you store shoes in their original boxes, label them clearly with a permanent black marker, so you can make finding shoes you want to wear a snap.

Finally, keep the floor of the closet clean. Once things start stacking up on the floor of the closet, chaos is imminent! I try to keep only two things on the floor of my closet: a laundry basket for dirty clothes and an empty box for things to give away.

Culling a Full Closet

I once went to a friend's house to pick her up to go out somewhere; she wasn't quite ready, so I went into her bathroom with her, to visit while she finished getting ready. As we chatted I took a peek into her closet and gasped: there was hardly anything there! A few shirts, a few dresses, and a few pairs of pants, that was all. Lots of empty rack space stretched across the closet.

"What happened to all of your clothes?" I asked, bewildered.

"Oh, Jim helped me clean it out. He encouraged me to give away everything but the things I really wear and enjoy wearing. I got rid of clothes I've had since college! But, even though my closet looks empty, you won't believe the freedom I feel!"

I was astonished. She had given up her excess baggage. Just like that. Everyone wants to do it, but my friend actually *did it*. Closet experts estimate that many of us wear only 10 percent of the clothes that are in our closets and drawers. My friend gave up the other 90 percent, and bought herself a tremendous amount of space and freedom in the process.

LETTING GO

Before you take such drastic measures, consider taking small, baby steps into the realm of effective closet management. Cleaning out closets doesn't mean you have to throw away all your old, disgusting, stained, favorite clothes that no longer fit. Just get rid of a *few* of them. Take baby steps.

When I first began culling through my closet, I set out a medium-sized empty box and tentatively began taking too-small, outdated, froufy clothes off their padded hangers. I folded the items carefully and put them in the box. I'd get two or three items in the box, then take one out. I only did this while my husband was at work; I knew he'd have no appreciation for my ability to agonize over every single item I contemplated putting into the box.

Once the box was halfway full, I'd had enough. My high school prom dress topped it off, and I took the box straight to my car. I knew I had to give it away quickly, so I put it in the back of my car, ready for the next run to Goodwill.

I went back up to the closet, culled the extra, empty hangers, and noticed something amazing: I could scarcely remember what I had just cleaned out and boxed up to give away. Oh, sure, I remembered the big, obvious pieces, like the prom dress and the size four leather skirt I had never been able to squeeze into. But the rest of it vanished from my memory as soon as it was removed from my closet. What was left instead was space—glorious space!

If it's been a while since you've seen a bare spot in your closet, it's time to clear things out a bit. I'm not asking you to give away all your clothes. To start with, set out a medium-sized box and put in it the things you haven't worn for two or more years.

If you have the skill and/or inclination, keep in mind that new life can be breathed into old garments, especially if they are made of high-quality material. Classic clothes that don't fit can often be restored to a glorious state of wearability with just a few simple alterations. Alternatively, outdated garments can be recycled: use them to make a tote bag, a quilt, placemats, braided rugs, chair mats, pillows or other home furnishings, or brew up a dye bath. The possibilities are endless. (Outdated formal wear, especially prom gowns and the ubiquitous bridesmaid dress, have special appeal for their morphability. Do you or anyone you know have a little girl in their lives? Pass on those dresses! With a few strategically placed safety pins they become exquisite dress-up clothes.)

As you cull through the closet, take a break when the box you're filling is full. Put it in your car and pat yourself on the back. In a week or two, do it again, but this time fill the box with things that haven't been worn in a year or more.

Once you realize that you truly don't miss the things you give away, and once you see how liberating the extra space is, you'll find that letting go of closet clutter isn't nearly as difficult as you'd feared. In fact, it can be a little bit addicting!

OLD BED LINENS

Now, let's talk about the linen elephant in the middle of the room, the ultimate storage hog, the old comforter that you're sick of because it's been on the bed for years. You buy a new one, but the old one is still serviceable so you can't bring yourself to throw it out or give it away. You keep it on hand, thinking that perhaps one day you'll want to put it back on the bed, or maybe you can use it as a picnic blanket!

An old comforter set, complete with matching bedskirt and pillow shams, can easily fill an entire shelf in a small closet. Give it up! Give the entire set to charity, to Goodwill or the Salvation Army. Consider it recycling, for that is exactly what it is. Old, unused items like these sap space and energy. A closet full of old linens that you will never use again is demoralizing. Give that stuff away and reclaim your space.

While you will no doubt want to hang on to high-quality down comforters or duvets, which can be renewed by simply changing the cover, go ahead and toss moth-eaten blankets, electric blankets that no longer work, and sheet sets that are stained or threadbare.

Laundry Cycle, Start to Finish

There are four steps to successful laundry maintenance. If you leave out any of the steps in the cycle, you are asking for trouble, setting yourself up to be overwhelmed by this common source of housework woe.

Here are the steps: (1) wash, (2) dry, (3) fold, (4) put away. That's it, but many of us get hung up on the last two steps. There's just something about a dryer full of clean clothes, needing only to be respun for a few minutes to fluff out the wrinkles, that invites us to stop before the laundry process is through. (More on this Clean Clothes Syndrome later....)

There's nothing more daunting than Laundry Day, where you first face a mountain of dirty clothes, then a mountain of clean clothes that need to be folded and put away. The trick is to break the large job up into smaller, more manageable tasks throughout the week. Do one small load of laundry a day, and you'll never have to face those daunting piles again.

Laundry is one area where "many hands make light work." One person in your household can throw in a load of clothes to be washed before leaving for work in the morning. Whoever's home first can put the clothes in the dryer. After dinner, everyone can pitch in to help fold and put clothes away. This is an easy, efficient system that can help tame those incessant, demanding piles of laundry.

LAUNDRY BASKETS GALORE

You can never have too many laundry baskets. I have about 10 of them, and they make life much easier around our house. When they're not in use, they stack neatly and don't take up much room. I keep at least one basket on the floor of each closet, where it acts as a dirty-laundry hamper. When it's time to do a load of whites, for example, I grab an empty basket and make the rounds, collecting whites from each basket, or I have everyone in the family tote their whites to the laundry room.

To really simplify things, keep two laundry baskets in the bottom of *each* closet. If space is at a premium, and it usually is in closets, then stack the baskets, one inside the other. Use the top basket to collect dirty clothes. When the basket is full, take it off the top and cart it to the laundry room, but leave the bottom basket in place, so you'll still have a place to put dirty clothes.

If you have two closets or a closet that is large enough for two side-by-side baskets, use one for light-colored clothes and one for darks, or buy a laundry sorting hamper with labeled bins for lights and darks to make things really easy.

Here is the key to quick, effective laundry organization: Once the clothes are dry, take them out of the dryer (or off the line) selectively, in an organized way. Start with the items that don't suffer from wrinkles—socks, underwear, towels—and put them in the bottom of the basket. Save the clothes that wrinkle easily until last: shirts and T-shirts, pants, and so on. Smooth them out immediately, then hang shirts and pants in your closet right away. What you're left with is a semi-organized laundry basket of clean clothes. The socks and towels and things that don't suffer from being wrinkled are in the bottom, while T-shirts and shorts and children's clothes and other items that need to be folded promptly are neatly piled and semi-folded on top.

Now fold the clothes, but wait! What's that? The phone's ringing, a child is crying, you're late for work, you have to run out the door and can't fold clothes right now. Don't worry, the basket is on autopilot thanks to the structured way you did something as simple as taking clean laundry out of the dryer or off the line and putting it in a basket.

TIP: *Fresh off the Line*

While electric clothes dryers are *de rigueur* in many places, such as the perennially soggy Pacific Northwest, there are many locales where line-drying is popular, and with good reason: nothing smells as sweet as clothes, sheets, and towels dried outdoors, in the fresh air and sunshine. In winter months, clothes hung indoors to dry can help humidify the house. Line-drying has the added benefit of dramatically reducing electric bills, too.

Clean Clothes Syndrome

You've conquered a mountain of dirty laundry, but the basket full of clean, folded clothes presents another challenge. Once the clothes are clean, you breathe a sigh of relief, but the fact is that the job is not over. Don't stop yet! Don't put off putting them away, or that nice clean basket of clothes will instantly turn to...clutter.

Baskets full of clean clothes are insidious forms of clutter. After all, the clothes are already clean, so it's all too easy to rationalize putting off the final step. It's just too easy to put that basket in a corner and forget about it (until you trip over it, or need to get a shirt out that just happens to be at the bottom).

Putting clean clothes away can be tedious, so the trick is to do it quickly and get it over with. Once the dirty clothes have been laundered, put the clean, folded clothes back into the laundry basket and take it back to the room, then put the clothes away *promptly*. Then put the empty basket back in the closet, or wherever you keep it, ready to receive a fresh batch of dirty clothes.

Families, especially, seem prone to Clean Clothes Syndrome. "We always have clean clothes," says Ed, the married father of three in West Chester, Pennsylvania. "There are always three or four baskets of clean clothes at the top of the stairs. We can get the clothes clean, but we just can't seem to get them put away!"

I know this syndrome well. I suffer from it myself upon occasion. When things get crazy around the house, it's all too easy to get the clothes clean and folded and put the basket in the room where the clothes belong, and then...leave it there.

A variation of this syndrome is even more insidious: the Disorganized Heap of Clean Clothes Variant.

Byron, also a married father of three who lives in North Carolina, is in charge of keeping the family's clothes clean. "Both my wife and I work, and with three young children, keeping the clothes clean is about the best we can manage." So he washes the family's clothes, dries them, then tosses them onto the guest room bed, where they lie in a heap. The whole family retrieves the clothes they wear from the heap. Nothing is ever folded. Lots of ironing is required.

Both variants of the Clean Clothes Syndrome can be addressed with two simple changes in the household routine: (1) the whole family needs to pitch in, and (2) they need to do a little bit every day.

Enormous piles of clean clothes, folded or not, can overwhelm even the most stoic among us. When the clean clothes begin to pile up, say this to your family brightly: "After dinner tonight we all need to pitch in to put away these piles of clean clothes."

That's it. That's all you do. No TV or talking to friends on the phone or spending time on the computer until the clothes are put where they belong. It takes about 15 minutes, on average—maybe a bit longer if you have young children—then the problem is gone. If the clothes have not yet been folded, then designate one person to fold while the others put things away.

This team-based approach is really the only fair way to deal with the problem of getting the family laundry done. One person doesn't get all these clothes dirty, so one person shouldn't have to be responsible for getting them all clean.

TIP: *Drip Dryer*

Suspend a rod above the washing machine and dryer so you'll have a place to hang clothes as soon as they come out of the dryer. An added bonus: you can hang delicates that need to drip-dry directly over the washing machine, which can collect drips.

Seasonal Laundry Tips

Spring: Laundry tends to be lightest during the spring, with the exception of heavily soiled clothes worn in the garden or on the playing field. Thwart these laundry beasts by placing an empty, clean laundry basket *in the laundry room* so that heavily soiled garments can go directly into the basket, instead of dropping bits of soil and mud all over the house on their way to the bedroom or bathroom. Also, have kids put on play clothes before heading outside to play.

Summer: Summer clothes tend to be thin and lightweight, which is good, but the bad news is that they also tend to be stained with dirt, grass, oils, and perspiration. When gearing up for the demands of summer laundry, make sure you are well equipped with ample supplies of detergent, bleach, stain removers, and baking soda. Use an old toothbrush to loosen ground-in dirt. To remove grass stains, rub the stain with a bar of ordinary white soap, or try pretreating the stain with rubbing alcohol or molasses, an old folk remedy that often works.

Fall: Many of the substances that adhere to fall wardrobes are invisible: allergens in the form of airborne spores, mold, and pollen. If you or someone in your family suffers from respiratory allergies, then you'll want to take extra precautions in the fall and launder clothes after they have been worn outdoors, whether or not they are visibly "dirty."

Winter: Winter clothes tend to be bulky and difficult to clean. A washer can't hold too many sweatshirts, jeans, and thick cotton sweaters before it's full. Wearing undergarments such as long-sleeved T-shirts or turtlenecks beneath sweaters can dramatically reduce the amount of laundry you do in the winter; make sure other family members do the same.

20 Stain-Busting Secrets

1. Allow chemicals and enzymes to do the work. Pretreat stains with stain removers, then allow the garments to sit for the suggested length of time, usually 10 or 15 minutes, before laundering.

2. Tend to stains immediately after they occur instead of letting them sit. The longer a stain remains on fabric, the more difficult it will be to remove. Particularly with upholstery, spot-clean as soon as you notice small dabs or drips of food or other foreign substances.

3. Match the cleaning product and treatment to the stain. Treatments vary widely, so if in doubt it's best to check a laundry guide. (For example, heat and soap can set a stain that could otherwise have been removed by dousing with enzyme wash or soaking in cold water.) Several useful laundry guides can be found online, including www.FabricLink.com, www.GoClean.com, and www.CloroxLaundry.com.

4. Head stains off at the pass by only buying clothes that hide stains well. Trying to choose between an all-white mohair sweater or a dark, nubby plaid? Go for the plaid every time.

5. Remember, bleach is your *friend*. Adding a cup of bleach to a load of whites will keep clothes bright. Add the bleach when the washer is full of water, just before the cleaning cycle begins. (Use caution when washing delicates, however; chlorine bleach can degrade elastic and Lycra and cause yellowing. When in doubt, check the label.)

6. Because shampoo is formulated specifically to dissolve body oils, it does a great job of removing ring-around-the-collar. Keep a bottle by the washing machine.

7. Ball-point-ink stains can be removed by saturating the stain with hair spray, letting it dry, then laundering as usual.

8. Stop household stains before they start. Keep high-quality entry mats outside every exterior door, and another good mat or rug inside to catch as much foot-traffic debris as possible, before it has a chance to land on your carpets or rugs.

9. If you have a fluffy dog or cat, keep the fur around their paws well trimmed, which will minimize the amount of dirt they track indoors.

10. Bathe pets or have them groomed regularly, and give their coats a good daily brushing. Keeping your pets clean will help keep the rest of the house clean, too. (If you have a pet that is reluctant to self-groom, wet a kitchen towel and give your pet a quick rubdown. Having damp fur encourages both cats and dogs to spiff themselves up a little.)

11. If your pet has an "accident" on your carpet, upholstery, or clothing, deal with the mess right away; for specific tips on removing pet stains, see Chapter 10.

12. In many cases a stain will lighten with repeated washing. Plan on washing extra-dirty clothes twice—and be sure to pretreat those stains!

13. If something spills on a garment but you're not ready to wash it, pretreat the stain, then put the whole garment in a bucket of cold water until you're ready to wash it.

14. To remove a red wine stain, wet the stain with water, then add a layer of table salt. Rub and let sit five minutes. Then, pull the stained fabric across a heat-proof bowl, put it in the sink, then pour a pot of boiling water through the stain from a height of two or three feet. The combination of heat and pressure will eliminate the stain.

15. For stained or very dirty clothes, use the heavy duty cleaning cycle on your washing machine and add a little extra detergent.

16. Blood stains can often be removed by dampening or soaking the stain in cool water, then applying meat tenderizer, which contains enzymes similar to those used in some stain removers. Let it sit for 10–15 minutes, then launder as usual.

17. If you accidentally drip something on your shirt or pants and can't treat the spot right away, discreetly dab the spot with saliva, which contains enzymes that will begin breaking down the stain.

18. To remove lipstick or makeup stains, dip a cotton swab in non-oily makeup remover and dab the spot until it disappears.

19. To get stained socks and undergarments white again, put them in a pot of boiling water to which one cut-up lemon has been added. Turn off the heat, then let cool. Launder as usual.

20. For stains on denim or other heavy fabrics, wash similar items along with the stained article of clothing. The abrasion during the wash cycle will help loosen dirt and stains.

PUTTING STAIN REMOVERS TO THE TEST

One day, dismayed by a pile of freshly washed white clothes that still bore tell-tale perspiration stains (and worse), I decided to perform an old-fashioned experiment to test a few stain-removing products that promised on the label to work on clothing stains. I applied Out! Pet Stain and Odor Remover to one set of stained garments, Gonzo Stain Remover to another batch, and treated yet another batch with plain, white vinegar. I used Spray 'n Wash on a pair of impressively stained socks. I allowed the stain removers to sit for 15 minutes, then laundered them as usual with detergent in hot water, plus a generously-sized scoop of OxyClean. The end results were disappointing: none of the stains were removed or even significantly lightened.

It was time to bring out the big gun: straight Clorox bleach. Having suffered through a few unfortunate incidents with bleach, I generally resort to it only under extremely dire situations, and this was one of them. If the bleach didn't work, I was going to have to go out and buy new T-shirts, socks, and underwear. The stains were that bad.

Into the washing machine the still-stained clothes went, along with hot water and a lot of bleach. Not just a mere cup—several cups. Like, about three. As the machine began to churn the room filled with that distinct chlorine smell, like a swimming pool in summer. Once the cycle ended I eagerly pulled the clothes out and…

Ta dah! Success! With the exception of a few underarm stains that were so ingrained that the fabric was actually a thickened yellow solid in spots, the stains were gone and the brilliant whiteness of the clothes, especially the socks, was restored.

The bottom line? If you have stained whites, don't waste your time or money on stain removers. Use bleach instead.

Chapter Six

COMMON LIVING AREAS

The family room, or living room, or great room, or whatever you call the central room in your house, presents its own set of challenges if you want to keep a modicum of order in your home. More than any other room (except, perhaps, the kitchen), this is the room where every individual family member contributes to the mayhem.

The living room takes on an added burden when there are children in the house. From toddlers to teenagers, kids by definition carry with them and usually leave behind them a comet tail of stuff.

The key to outwitting the living room is twofold: you've got to *stay on top of it,* and you've got to *enlist the infantry.* You can't do it by yourself.

Stay on Top of It

Doing a little bit each day to keep this room straight is much easier than allowing it to degenerate into a quagmire and then gazing helplessly about, not knowing where to begin.

Staying on top of the living room is much easier if you reduce the amount of IWAH (Items Without a Home). IWAH are the bane of everyone trying to keep the house straight. These are the items that don't fit into any discernible category, or items that have special needs or are awkwardly sized.

In many cases the problem with having an abundance of IWAH can be solved by mentally redefining a few categories. You either need to decide what an item is and where it should go, or get rid of it.

As we've said before, flat, empty surfaces just beg to have IWAH plopped down on them. In my family room the offending space is a built-in desk. It attracts daily piles of IWAH. Right now, the desk is covered by a difficult-to-store jewelry-making kit (it can't be tilted upright, or all the color-coded beads will fall out of their slots and become disorganized), some giant room decals that need to be returned to Home Depot, a stack of library books that need to be returned, a few catalogs that I need to order from, a bag of party favors from a friend's birthday party (held two weeks ago), and a digital camera.

Where to begin?

Getting rid of several of these items depends on my needing to run a few errands, so the first thing I need to do is group those items together and find a place for them. I have a basket in the laundry room that I use for containing "errand items": into the basket go the decals and library books.

I have my daughter take the bead kit to her room. Storing it doesn't need to be my problem: I'll let *her* find a place for it. I can help her with it

later by helping her actually *use* the kit—the only sure-fire, mutually ac-
ceptable way to get rid of the darn thing.

I put the catalogs in the catalog basket (while I'm there I spend two
minutes and pull out some old ones to throw away), put the camera in
the drawer where it belongs, and throw away the bag of party favors. No
one will miss it.

A Place for Everything

The key is in putting things where they belong, then finding suitable solutions for items that don't fit neatly into any one category. There are
several techniques you can use for containing these types of items:

✦ The judicious use of baskets and other types of containers
makes straightening this room—or any room, for that matter—
go much more smoothly. A pile of random objects placed in a
decorative basket is magically transformed from a pile of clutter into a contained collection. Put attractive baskets in the
places where IWAH tend to collect. Then—this is key—empty
the basket regularly. Find a home for the items that have been
tossed into the basket, or throw them away.

✦ In many cases IWAH tend to be useful items we use every day,
such as loose change, pens, pencils, and pads of paper. We keep
them around because they are useful. Unfortunately, when they
are not being used, they amount to clutter. Find a place to put
these items.

✦ A small, round, glass container—a decorative goldfish bowl—
filled halfway with decorative marbles or glass stones is an attractive way to store writing implements. To further streamline
the effect, spend a dollar or two and buy a package of 10 matching ballpoint pens. Keep mismatched freebie pens in a drawer,
or throw them away. Keep the bowl of pens on a desk or
counter, and store pads of paper in a nearby drawer.

✦ Location is everything when dealing with IWAH. Look at your drawer space as real estate: centrally located, easily accessible drawer space is valuable, but the temptation is to fill these centrally located drawers with odds and ends because they are convenient. Spend a few minutes each day cleaning out these prime-real-estate drawers.

✦ Another way to make use of valuable drawer space is to use drawer dividers, which keep the space from becoming a disorganized bin of chaos.

✦ Keep in mind that IWAH may be small and seemingly insignificant, but they add up quickly and can soon overwhelm.

✦ Designate storage areas for similar-type IWAH that you tend to run across repeatedly. If you tend to run across random photos, for example, then buy a photo storage box and keep it in an easily accessible location, so runaway photos can be easily contained.

✦ The most insidious form of IWAH: paper. Loose papers that don't fit neatly into an organizational system or that you "may need soon" are among the most threatening types of clutter. Chapter 8 deals with specific strategies for managing paper, but in the meantime designate an easily accessible storage area for paper IWAH, an "In Box" that can visually contain the clutter.

OTHER CONTAINMENT STRATEGIES

As you set about organizing the living room, take a moment to analyze the space. Determine the big offenders, the items that tend to keep this room messy. Here are some typical big offenders and some strategies for coping with them in an efficient way:

✦ **Catalogs and magazines.** By their very nature these items multiply: you don't have to lift a finger. Publishers and catalog companies send them to you automatically every month and sometimes every week. Set aside a basket to contain magazines and catalogs, and when a new issue arrives, toss out the old one. If you want to hold on to a particular issue, use magazine storage containers that are designed specifically for storing these items neatly. Or, clip just the articles you want to save.

✦ **Books.** Books also threaten to overwhelm many living rooms. If books tend to clutter this space, invest in a bookcase that can keep them contained. The trick is to avoid using the bookcase for knickknacks—photos and candles and figurines that can proliferate and keep the space from being used more efficiently. (For tips on keeping an uncluttered bookcase, see Chapter 2, "The Essential Bookshelf.")

✦ **CDs, DVDs, and videos.** Unfortunately, even organized, contained forms of electronic storage media add quite a bit of visual clutter to many family rooms unless these items are kept out of sight, stored in closed containers or behind doors. A storage unit that contains shelves for books and magazines, plus shelves with doors that can contain CDs, DVDs, and videos, can often solve all these storage needs.

✦ **Newspapers.** At best, neatly stacked newspapers make a room look disheveled. At worst, scattered piles of newsprint litter the room, covering tables, chairs, sofas, and even the floor. If you're after a streamlined look, removing old newspapers immediately is the first step. Make it easy. Keep a recycling bin in the kitchen, utility room, or in a nearby closet. Make the offending paper easy to toss.

✦ **Toys.** No one wants to be banished to a remote corner of the house, and this includes kids. Unless you have teenagers, kids are likely to want to play and congregate in parts of the house where they are likely to run into others. In most cases this means the family room. Make it easy to collect toys by placing a large, decorative storage bin in an inconspicuous spot, such as behind the sofa or tucked beneath an end table.

Now, spend five minutes every evening straightening common living areas before bed. Throw away the newspaper, put dirty drinking glasses in the dishwasher, put toys in their designated storage container, straighten pillows, fold sofa throws, and get the room ready for the next day.

Lending Library

Q: I have an extensive collection of CDs and DVDs and my friends often ask to borrow from my collection, but I seldom get them back, then I forget what I lent to whom. Is there an easy way to solve this problem?

A: Absolutely. My friend Kathryn Dickinson and her brilliant husband Bob have devised an ingenious solution for keeping track of the many CDs and DVDs they lend to friends. They created a "Dickinson's Lending Library" sheet on their computer that has a column for the title, date, and person to whom they lent the item, then a column to check when the item is returned. They put the sheet on a clipboard and hang it on a wall in their media room, next to their extensive library of literally hundreds of titles. "I don't mind lending things now because I have a way to keep track of who has what," says Kathryn. An added bonus: friends who have already borrowed titles can glance at the list and be reminded of titles they need to return without Kathryn or Bob having to say a word!

You can use this system with any type of item you are frequently asked to lend: books, tools, and children's videos can all be accounted for easily with this system.

ENLIST THE INFANTRY

Remember, you didn't get this room out of order by yourself, so you shouldn't have to straighten it by yourself, either. Before kids go to bed, have them put away their toys. Older kids can take drinking glasses to the kitchen or help fold sofa throws. (Remember, this isn't intensive cleaning. There should be no dust rags or glass cleaner involved. This is just basic straightening, which will, by the way, make cleaning much easier when that is the task at hand.)

Too Much Stuff?

The living room is not a great place to store collectibles. This is a room that tends to attract a lot of transient clutter, items making their way from one room to another (like shoes) or items on their way to the recycling bin (like cans and newspapers). You can help keep this room looking presentable by minimizing the number of doohickey décor items.

If you simply must store your Lladros in the family room, invest in a special display case that will keep the collection contained and dust-free. A wall-mounted display case is a great way to use space wisely. Small figurines can be safely stored in a glass-topped display table that can do double-duty as an end table.

Start Smart with Forgiving Furnishings

There's an art to decorating with minimal cleaning in mind. If you find yourself falling in love with and then contemplating the purchase of a white suede sofa, for example, then have a caring friend forcibly remove you from the store before you commit yourself to such an impractical, high-maintenance furnishing.

This is not to suggest decorating with plywood and burlap. (*"But it does such a great job hiding dirt!"*) There *is* a happy medium.

We once bought an older house that had just been outfitted with brand-new carpeting. In mauve. We hated it, but couldn't afford to replace it, so what genius thing did we do next? We bought blue-and-mauve plaid sofas, to match!

We soon discovered that the pale plaid didn't do such a great job of hiding stains. Our brand-new baby helped us with this discovery. It wasn't long before we moved again, but in the meantime we were stuck with not inexpensive, stained sofas in a fabric we didn't like and a color we didn't wish to carry over into our new abode. So we very sensibly had the offending sofas slipcovered. This time we did a better job picking fabric. We weren't just looking for a color we liked; this time we were considering texture and weave, too. We took home samples and carefully considered our choices. We finally settled on a neutral, mossy green fabric with a basketweave texture. It took the seamstress a few weeks to make the slipcovers, but when they were ready, we put them on and our life immediately became much easier. This is not an exaggeration. The new fabric wore like iron. The slipcovers weathered unimaginable abuse at the hands of my two young children, their pets, their friends, and their father (not to name names), but no matter what abuse the family doled out, the fabric looked brand new.

And then came the ultimate test: two kids with a nasty stomach flu.

Into the washing machine the slipcovers went. I held my breath. Once they were freshly laundered, I put them back on and...cried. Tears of pure, undiluted joy streamed down my cheeks. The slipcovers were beautiful. They still fit, the color hadn't faded, the nap of the fabric held its own. The sofa battle was over, and I had won.

TIP: *Avoid This at All Costs!*

In many living rooms the visual clutter is a result of many items being crowded into a space that is too small, such as the mantel. If you store things on your mantel, such as photos, books, dried flower arrangements, candles, or trophies, make sure that you do *not* have a mirror hanging behind the collection. A mirror over the mantel visually doubles the number of items kept there.

A better way to use mirrors: when you want to add reflected light and a sense of space (but only if the area in front of the mirror is kept free of clutter), or when you want to make something look larger, such as a flower arrangement.

THE MORAL OF THE STORY

If you make good, solid, practical furniture and fabric choices, keeping the living room looking good becomes much easier. If you can't buy new furniture or slipcovers, buy plastic furniture protectors and give up wearing shorts in the summer: you'll stick to the plastic (I'm *kidding*). But, seriously, if you can't afford new furniture or slipcovers, toss a decorative throw over delicate or pale fabrics to help provide a barrier against wear, sunlight, and stains.

Another great place to do a little preemptive, dirt-defying, stain-hiding decorating: the floor. Cover pale or light-colored carpets with strategically placed rugs. Make sure the coffee table rests on a dark, patterned rug that can protect the carpet and hide stains equally well. (You'll find more on "forgiving" flooring choices in the next chapter.)

If you are in the market for new tables—end tables, coffee tables, sofa tables, any tables at all for the family room—keep in mind that wood is more forgiving than glass. It does a better job of hiding dirt and fingerprints, although it can be easily marred by water rings from glasses, bottles or cans, so be sure to keep drink coasters handy. Figure out which type of material better suits the needs of your family.

THE COFFEE TABLE DILEMMA: WOOD OR GLASS?

Coffee tables and end tables in family rooms tend to take a lot of abuse. Although some wood finishes can be less forgiving of beverage rings and stains, scratches and nicks in wood are much easier to repair or disguise than heavily scratched glass, which also tends to show fingerprints and dust more readily than wood. Another tip: Look for tables with built-in storage, such as drawers or baskets beneath the table top.

So, which will it be, wood or glass?

Choose wood if:

✦ You have small children who tend to leave sticky fingerprints everywhere

✦ Dusting is not your strong suit

✦ Your family uses the coffee table for eating or playing games

✦ Someone in the family has poor vision (so they won't stumble into the table)

Opt for glass if:

✦ The room is small and you want to create an illusion of space

✦ Family members tend to leave cans, bottles, or drinking glasses on the table

Finally, save wood furniture throughout your home by providing coasters or, better yet, a selection of sweat-proof drinking cups for your family to use for cold or iced beverages. These insulated cups trap moisture between layers of plastic and keep it from puddling around the bottoms of drinking glasses and causing condensation stains.

FAST FIXES FOR SMALL SPACES

As a rule, it's best to avoid furnishing a small space with large, bulky furniture. Keep the furniture scaled in size to the proportions of the room. If you're looking for drama, opt for low backs, open arms, and curvy shapes as opposed to pieces with visual heft and bulk.

In small spaces, it's helpful to have some pieces that can multitask. Look for end tables with some storage capacity, for example, or use the back of a door for additional hooks or to hang a bulletin board. A sofa can contain a guest bed, and an ottoman can store out-of-season clothes. Look for ways to make small spaces work overtime.

How to (Easily) Clean the Living Room

As elsewhere, the primary rule is to *straighten before you clean*. If you have done a good job of enlisting the infantry, this should not be difficult. Put away large items first, then move on to smaller items. This will give you a nice, hefty dose of instant gratification, which will keep you going until you're done. Fluff pillows, fold or smooth sofa throws, straighten magazines.

Then, *remove trash*. Many living rooms are without that most basic tool of mess management: the waste basket. If you have room, put one in the living room big enough to contain newspapers, magazines, cans, bottles, and other odds and ends destined for the recycling bin, along with a smaller waste basket for tissues and other trash.

Next, *clean surfaces*. In the ever-improving world of home-cleaning products, great strides have been made in the area of dust-removal products. It seems as though the entire industry has declared war on dust, making it as easy as possible to dust quickly and efficiently. Pop-up wipes preloaded with furniture polish make dusting very easy—so easy a child can do it (hint, hint).

If these products strike you as just a bit ridiculous—not to mention not exactly environmentally friendly—then a clean, damp rag works just as well (maybe better, because you can use the damp rag to quickly swipe books, pictures, and knickknacks as you go).

Because so many people tend to congregate there, the living room tends to rapidly accumulate evidence of humans; namely, fingerprints.

A few squirts of glass cleaner and well-placed swipes will go a long way toward dramatically improving the appearance of this room.

Finally, *clean the floors,* making a quick run-through with the vacuum cleaner (see next chapter), and you're done.

QUICK 5: CLEANING THE LIVING ROOM

1. Put away IWAH, and take leftover food, plates, mugs, and drinking glasses back to the kitchen.
2. Straighten pillows and sofa throws.
3. Throw away any trash or old newspapers.
4. Dust with a damp rag or disposable wipe, straightening as you go.
5. Vacuum high-traffic areas and remove any visible dirt or debris on the floor.

TIP: *Let There Be Light!*

Before you clean a room, turn on all the lights. In a well-lit room you will be able to see dust, dirt, and cobwebs that otherwise would have gone unnoticed. And here's a great tip: the best time to dust a room is when sunlight is streaming in at an angle, which illuminates every speck of dust on polished wood surfaces. If you suddenly notice dust as the sunshine streams into a room, grab a dust rag or premoistened quick wipe and get to work!

How to Dust: The Basics

Always dust with something damp—a soft rag moistened with a very small amount of either water, lemon oil, or mineral oil to which you have added a fresh squeeze of lemon. Dry-dusting does nothing but move the dust around. When you dust, always work from top to bottom, letting gravity work for you, then vacuum last.

Pay close attention to the sources of dust in your home. I once bought a green velour sofa throw, and I soon began to notice as I dusted that the dust I was collecting had a greenish hue—the same color as the new throw. It didn't take me long to find another, less messy blanket.

Minimize the sources of dust in your home. Common big offenders include (ironically, for those allergic to dust) boxes of tissues. Keep tissue boxes to a minimum, and keep them in places where you can easily manage the dust they contribute, such as a kitchen counter that is frequently wiped down. Electrostatic filters can also greatly reduce the amount of dust in your home. Change the filters every three to four months for maximum efficiency.

If your house is particularly dusty or if allergies are a problem, consider replacing wall-to-wall carpeting with hardwood floors, tile, or even a very low-pile carpet such as berber. While carpeting is comfortable, it adds tremendously to the amount of dirt and dust in any house. Area rugs are easier to shake, beat, wash, or have cleaned on a regular basis.

For a quick and easy way to get rid of dust, lint, and pet fur on furniture, try EverCare's Large Surface Lint Pic-Up ($13, 800-435-6223). This large roller does for furniture what smaller versions do for clothes: it picks up stray bits of lint and fur with a sticky roller, and when one sheet is full you peel it off and have a fresh one underneath.

TIP: *A Quick Fix for Dirty Blind Cords*

Blind cords can become dingy in a hurry due to oil and dirt that are transferred to the cords every time the shade or blinds are pulled. Here's an easy fix: hold a dry towel behind the cords, then spray with an all-purpose carpet

cleaner. Let the cleaner sit on the cords for five minutes;
then, using a clean rag moistened with warm, sudsy water,
run the rag up and down the cords until the dirt is gone.

Fast Fireplace Fixes

Fireplaces are one of those home additions that can either provide a cozy backdrop to a chilly winter evening…or can accessorize the living room with a dusty, smelly, stale pile of ashes. If you have a stinky pile of ashes on your hands, here's how to clean it up quickly and efficiently:

First, snap on a pair of strong rubber gloves. Spray a fine mist of water over the ashes before you begin and as you clean, which will keep ashes from becoming airborne. Add a squeeze of lemon to the water to freshen things up a bit as you go. Shovel ashes into a heavy plastic bag, misting with lemon water often if things get too dusty. Sweep the fireplace clean, then use your vacuum cleaner attachment to remove the last stubborn dust particles. When you're finished, you can spread the ashes in the garden, to help make the soil less acidic.

If you are cleaning the fireplace seasonally, bidding goodbye to winter and welcoming spring, put a fresh, leafy plant in the fireplace, which adds a nice, green touch and serves as a nonverbal reminder to others in the family that the season of roaring fires in the fireplace is *over*, so don't even *think* about building another fire here—the fireplace has already been cleaned!

Finally, instead of building big, roaring fires in your fireplace, consider filling the space with an assortment of different sizes of scented pillar candles. When the candles are lit the effect is subdued and elegant, and the cleanup is virtually nonexistent.

Finally, keep in mind that a smoking chimney is a sign that creosote is building up, which is a major source of house fires. If your chimney is smoking, put out the fire and have the chimney cleaned *pronto*.

Scents and Scentsabilities

Keeping a living room smelling fresh can be quite a challenge. In extreme cases these rooms can take on the aroma of dogs, stale pizza, and sweaty gym socks. And that's not even during sweeps week or Superbowl Sunday.

The quickest fix is to grab a can of chemical room freshener, but, as with most things in life, the easiest fix is often not the wisest. Most room sprays and solid room deodorizers are loaded with carcinogenic compounds and formaldehyde, along with artificial fragrances. They are designed to both mask the offending odors and impair your ability to smell. Not a great solution. Here are a few safer but equally effective solutions that will freshen the air throughout your whole house, including the living room:

✦ When weather permits, make it a habit to throw open the windows and let fresh air freely circulate throughout the house. Stale, musty smells or cooking odors rapidly dissipate when fresh air is introduced. On sunny days that aren't too hot, open curtains and blinds and let the sunshine pour in.

✦ Musty odors often accumulate in the winter months. Combat stale smells by gently simmering lemon or orange peels in a pot of water on the stove, which will also add humidity to often-dry winter air. You can add cinnamon, cloves, or vanilla to enhance the gently wafting air freshener.

✦ A few drops of vanilla in a gently warmed oven will make the house smell like you've been baking all day.

✦ An open cup of vinegar placed next to the stovetop will help absorb strong cooking odors and keep them from circulating throughout the house.

✦ Essential oil diffusers are very effective for releasing soothing, healthful scents into the air. Most models have a compartment for water and a few drops of essential oil suspended above a light bulb or burning tea light. The heat causes the scent to be diffused. Stores such as The Body Shop and Bed, Bath & Beyond sell models that usually cost less than $20.

✦ Strategically located baskets of potpourri can add a gentle aroma to the air without resorting to harsh chemicals. Just be sure your potpourri is scented with all-natural essential oils.

✦ If you or someone in your house smokes, consider investing in a smokeless ashtray. Many can be found online; they usually retail for about $25. Some use filters, while others use ionization techniques to clean the air. Although these ashtrays don't do much to clean the air while a smoker is toting the cigarette or cigar around the house, they are very effective in capturing loose smoke when the cigarette or cigar is not being actively smoked. They also minimize the smell of a dirty ashtray, and many feature ash compartments that can be easily removed and cleaned in the dishwasher. Most run on batteries, so they're portable.

✦ If you simply can't give up the ease and quick results of room sprays, look for an all-natural citrus spray that uses a fine mist of citrus oil to help eliminate odors.

Chapter Seven

FANTASTIC FLOORS

For our purposes there are two basic categories of flooring: hard, bare surfaces such as wood, tile, stone, and vinyl, and softer surfaces such as carpets and rugs.

Outwitting Filthy Floor Surfaces

Floors can be tricky. They can get dirty in any number of ways. They can be cluttered with stuff, littered with dirt, dust, and debris, or coated with sticky, mysterious substances that glom onto socks and feet and paws and generally make floor life miserable. Keeping floors clean, then, with a minimum of effort requires a three-pronged strategy.

GET LARGE ITEMS OFF THE FLOOR

First, you've got to keep stuff from littering the floors. Shoes, toys, bags, umbrellas, backpacks, and stacks of books or papers are messy looking and virtually impossible to clean around. So take a look around your floors and take note of things residing there that need to find a more suitable home.

In many cases the large items that litter your floor can find a cleaner, more suitable place to stay if you simply hang them on hooks installed in strategically selected locations. A row of hooks in the laundry room will give people a place to hang coats, hats, scarves, backpacks, and pet leashes.

For items that don't lend themselves to being stored on hooks, such as gloves and shoes, a compact storage unit by the door can keep things tidy. If you and your family tend to remove your shoes when you come inside the house—always a good idea, by the way—then a strategically located shoe rack in the hall closet, entryway, or mud room will keep shoes from coalescing into an unsightly (and difficult to clean around) pile on the floor. I keep a hanging canvas shoe rack in the hall closet, so shoes stay neat, organized, and off the floor.

The most important area to keep clean and tidy is the hall or entryway around your front door. This is where visitors get their first impression of your home, and it's also the place where you are most likely to enter and feel an overwhelming sense of dismay if this area is strewn with miscellaneous shoes, book bags, umbrellas, toys, and other wayward items.

Many homes and apartments have a storage closet near the front door. Use this space judiciously. If the closet is small, and most of them are, then guard the closet carefully. Keep it organized. Use it for the items that tend to come through the front door and get plopped onto the floor. Don't allow this potential clutter-buster to become a repository for out-of-season coats and unused luggage. Put the things you seldom use in a less strategically located storage area.

Finally, if you have items that simply must be stored on the floor, then put them in clear storage containers, so the items they hold will be contained, orderly, and easily identifiable.

REMOVING DIRT AND DEBRIS

Once the large items have been removed, it's time to focus on dirt/hair/fur/dust/debris. Manual removal of these types of floor offenders can be labor intensive. You've got to vacuum or sweep to even make a dent in it (more on both of those later). So the best way to deal with this type of mess is to prevent it as much as possible in the first place.

Two small, simple behavior modifications can go a long way toward keeping your floors clean:

+ Place high-quality rugs or mats outside and inside each exterior door.

+ If you have an indoor dog or cat or two, you need to brush them every day. (If you have children, this is a great job for them.)

If you make these two small changes, you will see a dramatic improvement in the overall general cleanliness of your floors.

Another tip for keeping dirt and debris in check: when you notice a small bit of fur, bark, or mulch on the floor, pick it up! Don't wait to vacuum. This spot-cleaning will go a long way toward stretching out the time between needed vacuuming.

Finally, pay attention to the culprits that bring the dirt and debris into your home. In my case, it's usually the dog. Skippy has a gorgeous coat of long, soft, white fur, with particularly fluffy paws, which attract dirt like magnets. The solution? I regularly have the fur around his feet trimmed as short as possible. When the fluffy dirt magnets are well groomed, I deal with a lot less filth on my floors.

DAMP-MOPPING TO MAKE FLOORS SHINE

I have a friend who damp-mops her kitchen every day. To me this seems excessive, though she swears that it takes her no more than five minutes, and, I must admit, her hardwood floors gleam like mirrors.

I'm a lot less likely to mop my floor than she is. My kitchen gets it every two weeks whether it needs it or not, although I do a lot of spot-cleaning in between.

Spot-cleaning? The kitchen floor? You bet.

As soon as something spills, splashes, or drips, wet a kitchen towel and give the whole area a quick wipedown. If I spill a drop of milk on the floor, I immediately wipe it up, and I get the adjacent three or four feet in all directions while I'm at it.

While I'm wiping up, I may notice a drip or spill left by someone else. I flip the rag over, dampen it some more, and wipe that area as well.

The end result is that, while my floor is rarely damp-mopped all at once, the parts of it that tend to catch drips and spills get wiped down a lot. They stay clean, even though I'm mop-a-phobic. Take *that*, filthy floors. You've been outwitted.

Choosing Floor Surfaces Wisely

Not all flooring is created equal. Ask any flooring salesman, or read an ad for flooring in a home-decorating magazine. Some flooring is lowly and cheap; other flooring is so expensive you might as well gild the floor in gold.

But wear, durability, and ease of care is not necessarily tied to price points. While it's true that a high-quality wool rug will wear better than a woven tiki mat, there are a lot of durable flooring materials available that won't break the bank.

Analyze the surface of your floors. If you have low-quality, light-colored wall-to-wall carpeting, then you are just asking for a lot of maintenance if you want your floors to look halfway decent.

Do you have pets? Children? Does your family tend to wear their shoes indoors? These are all factors that will aid in the wear and tear of whatever flooring surface you have. A few surfaces—ceramic tile, stone, and marble—will perform the best. Your other options, which include carpets, hardwoods, laminates such as Pergo, and vinyl, will all eventually show some degree of wear and tear, although in the case of hardwoods the wear and tear may not be a minus; some people like the distressed look, and a well-worn wood floor can add personality and charm.

Shop carefully and compare products and prices. You may find that a more durable floor may even be an affordable option. Ceramic tile, for example, can cost less than one dollar per square foot, though it wears like iron. There are some downsides, though: tile (and stone) flooring is much harder than other types of flooring materials. Fragile items that are inadvertently dropped on these surfaces will instantly shatter, and the hard surfaces can be tiring to stand on for any length of time. There are some ways around these issues: you can place area rugs in places where you do a lot of standing, such as work areas in the kitchen or laundry room. Consider these factors when considering the type of flooring you want: in the end, the material that you think *looks* the best may not be the best option. If you decide you'd rather sink your tootsies into a lush carpet, however, then consider spending a bit more than the builders' grade and invest in carpeting with a tighter weave. Frieze carpet features a tight, almost curly weave that makes it bounce back after being stepped on. The result is a truly "trackless" carpet that hides a multitude of sins. A high-grade carpet pad installed beneath the carpet can also extend its life and make it feel more plush and luxurious, too.

A new crop of durable, modular carpeting (also known as carpet tiles) is steadily encroaching on the $13.2 billion residential carpeting and rug market. People with children and pets are justifiably attracted to the idea of being able to replace a single tile without having to replace an entire room (or floor) of carpet should damage occur. Carpet tiles first became available in the 1960s, but they were quickly shunned by the residential market due to coarse texture, drab colors, and visible seams. Vast improvements have been made since then. Manufacturers now refer to carpet squares as "modular carpets" or "carpet systems." These new products are often ideal for covering damaged hardwood floors, or for use in basements, since many of the tiles come with a built-in rubbery pad that clings to the floor without glue and can be removed without leaving marks.

But no matter what you have for flooring, a more important factor than material is color. Take a chocolate-colored tweed carpet any day over solid white tile. Deep, mottled, and neutral tones hide dirt. White, light, and pastel shades highlight dirt and stains. For resale purposes keep carpet colors neutral, or at least stick to the same shade throughout the house. Tan and beige are good. Pinks and blues are risky. You get the picture.

The exception to the rule of choosing darker colors for floor coverings applies to rooms that are bathed in natural light, which will bleach dark carpets and make them look old and faded in no time. For rooms that receive a lot of sunlight, a better choice is ceramic tile. Again, mottled, darker finishes are best. I wouldn't wish a white tile floor on anyone, except maybe a shut-in who lives on the top floor of a walk-up and has nine white cats.

Rug Mania

No matter what floor surface you choose, be sure to cover that surface with strategically placed area rugs. Lots of them. A well-placed area rug serves several functions: it anchors a room visually, adding depth and interest, and, most important for our purposes, hides dirt, crumbs, and footprints beautifully.

When choosing an area rug, you'll want to coordinate colors with the rest of the room, but make sure the rug you choose is a darker hue than the surrounding fabrics, carpet, and paint. This is important from an aesthetic point of view: the darker rug color helps pull the disparate elements of the room together, along with hiding dirt and stains.

On the other hand, avoid dark, monochromatic rugs or rugs with bold blocks of solid color, which shows up any lint or other debris. Opt instead for a busy pattern: Oriental-style rugs are the gold standard when it comes to minimizing the amount of time you spend keeping your floor looking clean.

Finally, when you choose area rugs, do yourself a huge favor and opt for styles *without* fringe along the edges (see box). Fringe has a tendency to attract dirt and stains, get matted, unravel, and wind itself around rotating vacuum-cleaner innards. Just say no to fringe.

Place area rugs anywhere you wish to add comfort, a visual anchor, and camouflage for dust, crumbs, and dirt. Periodically vacuum or shake out the rugs under these hot spots, and you'll cut down on the frequency of having to mop or vacuum a whole room. Here are a few great places to use area rugs:

✦ In front of all exterior doors

✦ In front of sinks and vanities

✦ Beneath dressing tables or areas where makeup or hair spray are applied

✦ Down long hallways

✦ In laundry rooms

✦ Beneath sofas and coffee tables

✦ Beneath the kitchen table

✦ In front of the fireplace (hearth rugs should be fireproof, and always use a screen to keep dangerous sparks from flying)

The Fringe Solution

I had a patterned rug with fringe around the edges beneath my kitchen table for years. The fringe drove me nuts. No matter what I did, the fringe looked dirty and tattered. During a visit from my in-laws, I mentioned my dilemma to my mother-in-law. "Just remove the fringe," she said, and we both got a gleam in our eye. I retrieved two pairs of scissors and we got down on our knees and went to work. Within half an hour the bothersome fringe was gone, and I had a "new" rug. (Note, however, that this was a relatively inexpensive rug with machine-knotted fringe along the edge. Removing the fringe may not be a desirable solution for expensive rugs with hand-knotted fringe.)

Vacuum Cleaner Basics

I admit it: I'm a vacuum cleaner nut. There's nothing I love more in the whole wide world of home-cleaning appliances than a good, solid, well-made, heavy-duty vacuum cleaner...or two. (I actually have four vacuum cleaners, but I probably err on the side of excess in that department, or so my husband claims.)

When you buy a vacuum cleaner, there are a few basic things you want to look for. First, you want an appliance that fits the job for which it is intended. A heavy-duty carpet vac won't do much good on hardwood floors, vinyl, or tile, for example; the powerful motor will merely blow the dirt and dust around the floor before it can be suctioned up and away. A better tool for hard-surface floors is a smaller, more compact canister model. Save the Big Daddy carpet vacs for, well, carpet.

Another place that begs for a smaller model? Stairs. Unless you're the buff bodybuilder type, you probably won't be all that jazzed about wrestling with a two-ton upright on skinny little stairs. Use a lightweight model instead, preferably one that has a small but powerful suction head that can reach into tight corners. (To find a model that suits your particular needs, check out www.ConsumerReports.com.)

In general, upright vacs do a better job of cleaning carpets, while canister models do a better job on bare floors. Canister models often feature lots of specialty tools for cleaning everything from crevices to drapes to upholstery to mini-blinds.

The average household changes the vacuum-cleaner bag four times a year. Full bags can decrease the suction capability of your vacuum cleaner, so a good rule of thumb is to change them when the bag is three-quarters of the way full. To keep things smelling fresh, when you change the bag moisten a cotton ball with a few drops of perfume, cologne, or essential oil, then use the suction hose to vacuum up the cotton ball. It will go into the bag and keep things smelling fresh for weeks.

If allergies are a problem in your family or if your home tends to attract a lot of dust, invest in a vacuum cleaner that filters out tiny specks of dust and particulates: look for a model with a HEPA filter, which filters 0.3-micron particles at 99.97 efficiency.

What's the big deal about HEPA filters? HEPA stands for High Efficiency Particulate Air. HEPA filters have traditionally been used in hospital operating rooms, isolation wards, and pharmaceutical and computer chip manufacturing. Now they are more widely available in air-filtration devices and vacuum cleaners designed for home use. They are especially useful for those who suffer from allergies or other respiratory ailments, and HEPA filters are ideal for removing fine particulates from the air even for those who don't require the added cleanliness for medical reasons.

To give you an idea of how effective HEPA filters are, here is a breakdown of common indoor pollutants and their size:

Human hair: 80–100 microns

Dust mite waste particles: 10–24 microns

Mold: about 4 microns

Pollen: 10–40 microns

Bacteria: 0.3–50 microns

Asbestos fibers: 3–20 microns

Particles smaller than 10 microns are invisible to the human eye. The most common airborne particle size is 2.4 microns. The average vacuum cleaner filters particles from 30 to 50 microns, exhausting most harmful, respirable particles back into the air.

Watch out for flashy designer vacuums. As *Consumer Reports* magazine notes in a recent vacuum analysis, many newer models are all about show and little about suction. In many instances a higher price tag did not necessarily correlate with improved performance, although this tends to hold true for the models that cost more than $300. There aren't too many machines on the market for less, with the exception of smaller, hand-held models, that are both powerful enough to do the job *and* built to last.

Watch out for bagless-style vacuums that have a removable dirt container. In most cases removing and emptying the container spews enough dirt and dust back into the air so as to make that feature worthless. Another feature to be wary of: dirt sensors. Some of them are so sensitive that they can keep you vacuuming long after the floors are quite clean.

Recommending a specific brand is difficult; in many cases the performance varies greatly not from brand to brand but from model to model. For example, in the 2003 *Consumer Reports* evaluation of specific vacuum cleaners, Kenmore and Hoover had vacuum cleaners both at the top *and* at the bottom of the list. When shopping around for a vacuum cleaner, it's well worth the time and trouble it takes to do a bit of research before you make your decision.

> **TIP:**
>
> *Your Secret Weapon: A Vacuum Cleaner...with Attachments*
>
> When it's time to clean the floor, look no further than your vacuum cleaner, but only if your vacuum cleaner has attachments. If it doesn't, put this book down and go get yourself a vacuum cleaner with on-board attachments. You can send me a thank-you letter later, after you've used it a few times to suck up dirt, crumbs, fur, and hair from corners, edges, nooks, and crannies that a vacuum cleaner without attachments could only *dream* of reaching.
>
> What attachments are you looking for? You want a long, stretchy hose that attaches to a long, empty tube. The business end of the tube then accepts variously shaped dirt-sucking accoutrements that make cleaning floors, furniture, window sills, and even the interior of your car a breeze. Especially useful are attachments that can reach into narrow crevices or brush-and-dust along curved edges like baseboards. After you've had too much coffee you can even use the appropriate attachment to groom the cat or chase down buzzing insects that somehow made it inside. An added bonus: kids *love* using vacuum cleaners with attachments. At the point when your kids think vacuuming is fun, you've got it made.

A Lesson from the Japanese: Take Off Your Shoes!

Perhaps the single most effective way to reduce the amount of dirt that makes it inside is to have friends and family remove their shoes at the front door. In wetter climates, including the Pacific Northwest, this seems to be *de rigueur*; leaving your shoes on there, especially in the wet winter months, is a sure-fire way to track in a streaming trail of wet mulch, mud, and leaves.

The habit of removing your shoes at the door is easier to adopt if you consciously wear shoes that are easy to remove. And you probably won't need to say anything to encourage visitors to remove their shoes: most visitors who see a neat row of shoes lined up inside the front door will do as in Rome and take their shoes off, too.

Hardwood Floors: A Primer

If minimal floor maintenance is the idea, then a hardwood floor may be just what you need. Hardwood floors are elegant, easy to clean, and they hide dirt well. A high-quality hardwood floor can last a lifetime. If the floor is damaged or begins to show wear and tear, it can be sanded and refinished. Hardwood floors are softer than tile, which is important if you have babies or toddlers underfoot, and can make a difference in the kitchen if you spend much time standing over the sink or stove. Finally, hardwood floors are a godsend if you suffer from allergies. Dust, dust mites, fur, and other allergens are easy to sweep up, vacuum, or whisk away with a damp mop.

According to the Hardwood Manufacturers Association, there are two major types of hardwood floor finishes: *surface finishes* and *penetrating finishes*.

Urethane is the most common surface finish. When a urethane or polyurethane coating is applied, the floor takes on a uniform, high-gloss sheen.

The most common penetrating finish is wax. Wax-coated floors have a soft, silky feel, and the wood grain is detectable to the touch.

These two finishes are not interchangeable. You can't apply wax to a urethane-coated floor, and you can't apply a urethane finish to a wax-coated floor without first sanding off all remnants of wax.

The best way to care for a urethane-protected floor is by regular sweeping and regular mopping with a barely damp mop. Fine particles of sand, dirt, or grit will cause tiny surface abrasions that will dull the surface of the floor, so keeping the floor swept clean will extend the life of the floor. Take care not to drop things on urethane-coated floors. Dings and dents will crack the surface coating.

Never use furniture polish to clean a hardwood floor; the residue left behind can cause urethane finishes to cloud, peel, or bubble. Be careful when dusting furniture, too: Overspray can damage the floor surface, as can hair spray, which should never be used directly over a hardwood floor.

Little can be done once hair spray makes contact with a urethane finish. Let the spot dry, then wipe clean with a slightly damp cloth. Any remaining damage will probably need to be repaired by refinishing. (If you have hardwood floors in a room or bathroom where hair spray is routinely used, use an area rug to keep the floor beneath potential overspray covered, or spread a bath towel over the area before breaking out the Aqua Net.)

Waxed wood floors also need regular sweeping, to remove dirt and debris, though the Hardwood Manufacturers Association cautions against damp-mopping. Waxed floors should be spot-cleaned using a solvent-based floor cleaner or mineral spirits—nothing water soluble. Surface stains can often be removed using a very fine gauge of steel wool (1 or 0) or sandpaper (80- to 120-grit), then rewaxing the area using a high-quality floor wax. Once a good coat of wax has been applied, the floor should need only occasional buffing to keep it looking shiny and new.

For scratches, dings, and dents in waxed wood floors, rub the meaty part of a walnut or pecan into the damaged area, or use a commercial wood filler.

If wax builds up and the floor looks dull, remove the wax buildup with mineral spirits, then rewax. While this can be a big job, the payoff is substantial: your floor will look great and probably won't need additional maintenance for years.

DO PETS AND WOOD FLOORS MIX?

You don't have to choose between having pets and gorgeous hardwood floors, although there are some steps you can take to make the two more compatible.

In many cases, in fact, hardwood flooring is a great choice for people who have pets. Wood floors don't harbor pet dander, fur, fleas, mites, or other allergens. Many pets actually prefer the naturally insulated surface of wood floors, which stay cool in the summer and warm in the winter.

To keep wood floors from being damaged by pets, follow these tips from the Hardwood Manufacturers Association:

- ✦ Clip your pet's nails regularly.

- ✦ Sweep or dust-mop regularly—preferably several times a week—to remove dirt, grit, and fur.

- ✦ Choose food and water bowls that are difficult to turn over. Use a throw rug, kitchen towel, or cotton place mat beneath the bowls to absorb drips.

- ✦ Clean up water spills or pet accidents immediately.

For more tips on cleaning up after your pet, see Chapter 10.

How Often Do Floors Need to Be Cleaned?

The general rule to keep in mind is that *the more frequently carpets and floors are cleaned, the longer they will last*. But the idea here is to minimize the amount of time we spend cleaning, right? So, here are a few tips:

- ✦ For carpeted floors that tend to get dirty, keep a vacuum cleaner stored nearby. In my house most dirt gets tracked in by the back door, which is near the kitchen, so I keep a vacuum cleaner in the pantry, near an outlet. and It takes me about two minutes to plug it in and suck up debris right at its point of entry, before it can progress further into the house. I usually vacuum this area once a day, though there are rooms in my house, like the playroom, which has berber carpet, that only gets vacuumed about twice a month. Only vacuum the areas that need it.

✦ For floors covered in hardwood, tile, or linoleum, keep a dust mop in a nearby closet and swish it around the floor once or twice a day.

✦ Change the bag on your vacuum cleaner regularly, which will keep the suction good and strong, so when you do spend time vacuuming, you'll see results.

✦ Use a vacuum cleaner with a high-filtration (less than 1 micron), disposable bag. A high-efficiency bag holds the dirt and prevents it from being blown back into the room.

✦ Invest in professional, hot-water-extraction carpet cleaning (or steam cleaning) once a year. I usually have my carpets cleaned in the fall, after the kids have tracked dirt and leaves in all summer and before the holiday season begins.

✦ Develop a good, solid relationship with a local carpet-care specialist. Forget the big chains—you'll have better luck with a small, independently owned company where the proprietor will know you and will know your carpets. The guys that own their own equipment live and breathe carpet care. They know what special blend of chemicals to use on just about any type of stain you can concoct. And, when you have a particularly nasty spill or stain, these guys are worth their weight in gold.

✦ Avoid using powdered carpet fresheners, which add a tremendous amount of dust to the house and can eventually build up in carpets, making them look dusty and dull.

✦ Rotate furniture around the room at regular intervals to avoid tracks and paths of wear and tear.

✦ Keep food and drinks out of carpeted areas, especially if you have young children. If you have very light carpet, avoid serving red wine or punch at parties and social functions.

✦ *Never* use a rubber-, latex-, or vinyl-backed floor mat or rug on vinyl floors. The rubber backing can cause severe discoloration that is virtually impossible to remove.

✦ Spread a flat bed sheet beneath the ironing board when you iron, which will prevent starch overspray from globbing onto the floor below.

✦ Only buy house plants that don't shed, or stick with silk. Avoid ficus trees and leafy ferns.

TIP: *Keeping High-Traffic Areas Clean*

According to the Carpet and Rug Institute, high-traffic areas in highly populated facilities such as public schools should be vacuumed *at least* once a day. The frequent vacuuming keeps the fibers from getting too dirty and compacted. You may not have such heavy traffic in your home, but the principle still applies: vacuum high-traffic areas more frequently than low-traffic areas to keep the carpet looking good.

Chapter Eight

ORDER OUT OF CHAOS:
THE HOME OFFICE

It doesn't matter if you have an entire room devoted to the business of running a home (or running a business out of your home) or a corner of a desk devoted to the task: the paperwork required to keep a home running smoothly is something we all have to deal with.

Janet, a chef at a high-end restaurant in a large metropolitan city, lives in a small apartment in a trendy part of town. She doesn't have the luxury of a dedicated home office; instead, the papers and forms and bills and coupons and letters and notices get piled, ironically, on the kitchen table. "I'd love to entertain more," says Janet sheepishly, "but I can't until I figure out what to do with this mess."

Susan was a successful real estate agent who quit her job to stay at home with her three young children. Every day she prepares three meals, maintains the yard, takes care of two dogs and a cat, stays on top of the family's laundry, runs carpool, shuttles the kids to and from extracurricular activities in the afternoons, and keeps the house in order...but you should see her home office. It's a mess.

Janet and Susan are not alone in their inability to keep their home offices straight. Unlike other areas of the house, the home office is plagued by a particularly insidious form of clutter: paper. The dilemma and constant aggravation of where to put paper is where many of us run into trouble.

I feel particularly well-suited to shedding light and giving guidance on this mine-laden area of outwitting housework for several reasons:

1. I have worked from home for many years and have a tremendous amount of paperwork that I deal with on a regular basis. Articles, papers, books, and other types of research material regularly intrude upon what might otherwise have a prayer of being an organized, efficient work space.

2. I am not by nature an overly organized type of person.

3. I have found a system that works.

I learned the hard way what it is to pay the price of being disorganized. For years my idea of a filing system was doing my nails. Then, several years ago, my husband was preparing our tax return. He needed a few receipts for big-ticket items that I used in my business, things like a new computer, printer, and home-office furniture. I couldn't find them, and I looked everywhere. Zero, zip, zilch, they were gone, having disappeared into the mysterious piles of paper I had covering every flat surface in the office and most of the kitchen.

I never did find them; I must have thrown them away inadvertently, and the price of my lack of organization was steep. I lost the tax write-off, and, even worse, my husband was mortified. He looked around at my piles in disgust. All I could do was hang my head in shame. (As bad as my lack of organization was, I have a friend who was worse, once throwing away an actual *paycheck* by mistake.)

So, things had to get really bad at my house before I was sufficiently motivated to change my ways. For me, the suffocating piles and the lost receipts sent a powerful message to that feeble part of my brain that should have been in charge of organizing things: Get off your duff and *do something about this mess!*

I did. Progress at first was slow. It took me months and months to stumble upon a system that works for me. But along the way, taking baby steps, I made progress. I'll tell you how I did it.

Buried in Paperwork

The average disorganized person has more than 3,000 documents or pieces of paper at home, including everything from birth certificates to store coupons, according to "clutter consultant" Michelle Passoff. Further, too much stuff in the average American's home creates an estimated *40 percent* more housework.

Admitting the Problem

Like other types of addiction, a tendency to hang on to every shred and scrap of paper is a destructive habit. As I took a look around my house, I saw that I was literally *littering* my own home (and that of my family) with paper. Piles of newspapers and magazines choked tabletops and spilled onto the floor. Stacks of bills and papers on the counter had nowhere else to go. And I had an epiphany: would I rather suffer the pain of throwing useless paper away, or continue to suffer the indignity of living in litter? Once I viewed it that way, the decision was easy: I began throwing things away.

I started with the piles of magazines. Out of maybe a hundred magazines, I kept 10. I bought a magazine storage container and put it in my bookcase. Voilà! Now I have a place to archive magazines and catalogs that I want to keep.

For current magazines—the ones not yet read—I wanted to keep them accessible, but didn't necessarily want them fanned out on the coffee table. The solution? A basket by my reading chair. It keeps my current magazines and catalogs neatly contained.

The next step was critical: every month, when I receive a new magazine or catalog, I either throw the old one away or file it. The stack in the basket doesn't keep growing. Instead, the contents keep changing. If I find that I want to keep a magazine just for one article, I tear the article out carefully and put it in a file. Which brings us to the all-important subject of…

The Essential Filing System

If you don't heed any of my advice anywhere else in this entire book, listen to this: A simple, accessible filing system will change your life. I mean it. Disorganized, messy stacks of paper will disappear, and, importantly, will stay gone if you utilize this system of storing everything you want or need to save in hanging files.

First, you need to have a filing system that is easy to reach and simple to use. A filing cabinet is perfect; if you don't have one and space is limited, consider a rolling filing cabinet that you can pull in and out of a closet, or cover with a pretty tablecloth and use as an end table, if things are really cramped. Alternatively, you can use a milk crate to hold hanging files. It can be easily stashed beneath a desk when you're not using it.

But the trick is, you've got to use it. Make it easy to use. Don't have 50 file categories; if you have too many files you'll never be able to keep them straight and will end up either misfiling things or getting discouraged and not use the system at all. So, keep it simple.

Now, not everything goes into the hanging files. (This is my system, anyway. You can create your own, but if you're looking for a place to start, you can use mine.) Bills and monthly household paperwork have their own, separate accordion file. Every year in January I go to an office supply store and buy a 12-month accordion file organizer. I keep it on an easy-to-reach shelf and I pull it out when I sit down to pay bills. The stubs of bills go into the appropriate slot, and anything that I might need for tax purposes goes to the very front of the January file.

What about bills? When they come in I put them in an incoming mail tray. They all stay there, together, until I'm ready to pay bills. I keep a supply of empty envelopes, stamps, and a checkbook all there in the same tray. When it's time to pay bills all I need are my tray and my accordion file.

Everything else goes into hanging files, and I do mean everything. Make your file categories broad. Take a look at your stacks of paper and see what you're dealing with. Here are a few of my file categories:

- ✦ Auto Records
- ✦ Business Expenses
- ✦ Product Manuals
- ✦ Important Documents (things like birth certificates and car titles)
- ✦ Pets
- ✦ Insurance
- ✦ Investments and Financial Planning

+ Recipes

+ Scrapbook

+ Fun Stuff

I also have a file for each of my children, where I keep their school and medical records. I have files for my business: a file for each book I write, a file for articles I've written, and another file for article and book ideas. The point is to personalize your filing system to suit your needs, but don't make it too complicated.

For investment information, switching to online delivery of quarterly reports and prospectus-type of information can dramatically reduce this type of paper clutter.

As I was putting together my system, I noticed that I had several random pieces of paper that didn't seem to fit neatly into any of the categories I had. I had a certificate for a free dinner at a local restaurant, a roster of women in my book club, a coupon for a new health club that was opening, a clipping of fun things to do around town that I cut out of the newspaper, and a picture I tore out of a magazine of a bookcase I want my husband to build. Where to file these random things? Inspiration struck: I created a file that I labeled "Fun Stuff."

What you want to avoid is a Miscellaneous file that everything gets dumped into. I do have a Miscellaneous file, but it's almost empty. It's got things like a copy of a traffic ticket and a flyer for a local babysitter that a neighborhood teen posted on our door (hmmm, come to think of it, I should put that flier in our Family Notebook under "Babysitters.") What? I haven't told you yet about our Family Notebook?

The Family Notebook

The Family Notebook is the third and final part of this system for organizing your home. The notebook is not an integral part; it is not absolutely vital to the success of the system (as the accordion file and hanging files are). But, if you have children, the Family Notebook greatly simplifies the vast amounts of paperwork that come into the house that are related to kids, school, and extracurricular activities.

My life changed the day I compiled a Family Notebook. The concept of keeping everything together in one convenient, easy-to-use binder eluded me for years. I stumbled upon the idea and gave it serious consideration one day while reading a book about time management. I had seen personal organizers in office supply stores, but had never given them much thought; they seemed to belong to the domain of powerful men and women in suits, or realtors, or stockbrokers, but not *me*.

I first realized the value of the Family Notebook as I perused the aisle of personal organizers at an office supply store. I was determined to find out what all the fuss was about with these bulky personal planners. If everyone found them so darn helpful, then maybe I needed one, too.

The first thing I noticed as I meandered through dozens of organizers was that they are very expensive. Sure, the low-end models started at around $20, but they didn't provide much in the way of organizational help. The Big Daddy organizers were chock-full of organization aids, but they were enormous and very expensive—well over $100. And, most of the organizing capabilities they contained were geared toward a professional work environment, with places to insert business cards and hour-by-hour daily planning guides. Not exactly what I was looking for.

The mid-range planners had most of the organizational tools included, but they were smaller, obviously designed to slip into a briefcase but not large enough to contain 8 x 11-inch sheets of paper, which is the size of most school papers—what I grapple with on a daily basis.

I left the aisle shaking my head in bewilderment, and then I looked up. I was in the lowly, plain-paper binder aisle, and I got an idea. I needed something to contain 8 x 11-inch sheets of paper. I needed something I could customize. And I didn't want to spend a fortune. Bingo. I had found the solution to my household organization woes.

I bought a plain, white, loose-leaf binder, multicolored organizational tabs, and a package of clear document-protection sleeves to hold important papers, like the school year calendar and an Emergency Information sheet for babysitters to use in case of an emergency.

Once I began working on a system, I stumbled across www.OrganizedHome.com, a website that offers *free* printable forms for organizing your home. That was when I really began to see the possibilities of having an organized system for my family.

For example, I found an Emergency Information sheet on www.OrganizedHome.com. Until then my "system" for this type of information was a hastily scribbled phone number for the babysitter and making sure my kids knew to dial 9-1-1 in an emergency. Organized Home's Emergency Information sheet beat my system by a mile.

Next, I made tabs for each category of information that I wanted to contain in the notebook:

+ Family Message Center
+ School Information
+ Calendar
+ Phone Numbers
+ Activities
+ Babysitters
+ Money
+ Medical
+ Forms
+ Holiday Planner

The beauty of this system is that it is easy to customize. If you spend a lot of time and money on quilting, beekeeping, training for triathlons, or any other unique hobby or pastime, you can add a divider and keep all the important information you need together in one place.

Another benefit of this system is that is simplifies the process of keeping up with household tasks and organization for other members of the family, too. Now my husband, daughters, parents, and baby-sitters can all find information they need quickly and easily. This system has helped us all.

---

5 Sure-Fire Ways to Have a Messy Office

✓ Use your desktop as a parking spot for incoming mail and newspapers.

✓ Keep lots of personal mementos on the surface of your desk.

✓ Store household IWAH (Items Without a Home) in your office.

✓ Put off filing household papers indefinitely.

✓ Keep *everything*, "just in case."

Making Your Home Office Work for You

All too often the home office becomes a cluttered, crowded room that serves as an overflow room for everyone's stuff. Stacks of bills and mail are piled on the desk; books and magazines cover every square inch of available space; and, to top it all off, the room becomes dusty because it's hard to clean around so many piles of paper and clutter. There's got to be a better way!

There is.

Once the piles of paper are culled, sorted, and filed, you can move on to streamlining the rest of the office and making it truly functional. Getting rid of loose papers is just the first step. Once you've mastered that area you can move on to the next task, which is to throw away other useless, space-hogging paper items:

Things to throw away:

Old phone books

Duplicate books

Paperback books that have already been read

Hardback books you didn't enjoy reading

Out-of-date reference books or software (such as annual tax software)

Old financial plans that have been updated

Things to keep:

Current phone books and reference guides

Cherished books

Mementos, photos, and family keepsakes

Financial records for the past six years

Keepsake magazines

Once you've culled through the material in your office and thrown away what is old and unusable, the key becomes organizing what is left. Take a good, hard look around the room and notice what areas work well, what areas don't work so well, and what areas are complete and total disaster zones.

In any office where organization is a problem and piles of anything are present, you can be sure that adequate storage space is lacking. If your home office contains a desk and little more, then I can almost guarantee that it is a mess.

I stumbled upon this truth when my husband and I moved from a small house where my office was holed away in a spare bedroom, into a house with a phenomenal home office. The room was so large I used it as an office *and* a playroom—the kids could play at one end of the room while I worked at the other. But what made this room so functional as an office was the walk-in-closet-sized storage area behind my desk. A small school library could have been stored in that closet. It was enormous. And suddenly my office clutter problem was solved. The stacks on my desk disappeared. I had room for everything.

We moved again shortly thereafter and I lost my wonderful storage space, but I had learned a valuable lesson: when things get cramped in the office, more storage space is needed, whether it be in the form of a luxurious, oversized closet, or—more likely—having adequate file space and shelving.

The next house didn't have a dedicated office at all; I used a loft over the stairs, but I outfitted it well. I bought enough bookshelves to cover an entire wall, put a rolling file cabinet beside my desk, and was able to thwart the return of unwanted piles and clutter because, once again, everything had a place.

If desk space is at a premium, and it usually is, you can free up the usually wasted space beneath your monitor with a *monitor shelf*, a platform with a drawer and storage space that fits between your desk and monitor ($29.98, www.ShopGetOrganized.com).

QUICK 5: CLEANING YOUR HOME OFFICE IN A HURRY

1. Shelve all books that are out of place.
2. Neatly stack all paper in an empty milk crate or basket.
3. Dust desk and shelves with a microfiber cloth or disposable furniture wipe.
4. Vacuum or sweep the floor.
5. Straighten chair, keyboard, and mouse.

TIP: *Deleting Dust*

✓ To clean your keyboard easily and quickly, when it is turned off, use an Unger Mini Duster, a yellow felt keyboard cleaning contraption that reaches between keys with ease ($3, call 800-833-6100 for store locations).

✓ Use an all-purpose disinfecting wipe to clean the keyboard and monitor case (not the screen), as well as the phone and switchplates.

> ✓ Use a dry or slightly damp microfiber cloth to clean
>   your computer screen.

When it comes to keeping a home office streamlined and functional, look no further than the hard-drive on your computer. Regularly cleaning out old files, transferring memory-hog files onto disks or CDs, and running the disc defragmenter periodically can all make the time you spend in your home office smoother and more productive.

Make Your Office a Haven

Once things are organized, the next step is to surround yourself with favorite family photos, artwork or posters on the walls, postcards from favorite places you've visited—anything that makes you smile and encourages you to use the room and enjoy the time you spend in it. Make your office space a haven.

Other items that can cozy up your office space include homey furnishings in colors and fabrics you like, candles, and maybe a plant or two. A writer friend of mine keeps a desktop waterfall on the corner of her desk; the sound of water trickling is soothing to her as she works. But be careful to not overdue it on the knickknacks. You want this space to have positive associations, but you don't want it to be cluttered or difficult to keep clean.

If you're in the market for office furnishings, look for ergonomic functionality as well as aesthetic appeal. You want this space to look *and* feel good.

Specialty products abound for keeping the home office neat and functional. For example, if computer and phone cords lie in a tangle on the floor, bundle them together with the Wire Snake, a colorful bendy gadget that contains up to eight cords into one neat bundle ($9.99, The Container Store).

Finally, it is no fun to work in a dusty, dirty environment. Now that the piles are gone and knickknacks are held to a minimum, keeping things clean isn't difficult. Keep a container of pop-up furniture cleaning wipes in a desk drawer and give your desk and bookshelves a quick dusting when you're on the phone, on hold, or even if you just need to stand for a few minutes to stretch your legs. (My mother-in-law has honed this dusting-while-you're-on-the-phone strategy to an art form. She uses dusting wipes to dust window blinds as she talks on the phone. "It's mindless," she says, "and after I finish my conversation my blinds are all clean!")

When your home office is kept neat and organized you will discover that keeping your home running smoothly becomes much more feasible. You'll know where things are and will be able to put your finger on important documents at a moment's notice. Things won't be lost or "fall through the cracks." It's a much nicer, saner way to live!

Chapter Nine

AN ENTIRE CHAPTER DEVOTED TO— YOU GUESSED IT—KIDS

If you live by yourself, chances are good that the messes you make are containable. Controllable. But things get complicated quickly once children enter the picture. Let's jump right in and talk about ways to outwit the messes that only kids can make.

If you have children or grandchildren underfoot, then you are all too aware of the insidious, continual messes that children introduce

into the cleanest of homes. Like Charles Schulz's Pig Pen, most kids
have a way of bringing dirt and clutter with them, depositing it wherever they've been, taking it with them wherever they're headed. Having
kids around can be very frustrating to someone who is trying to maintain a semblance of a clean home.

If we're talking about babies or toddlers, the messes can be especially vexing. Here we're not talking about misplaced Barbies or stray
Reeboks on the floor. We're talking about spaghetti on the walls and
spit-up on the sofa.

Children require an extra dose of preventive maintenance, to be sure.
This means that you will have to carefully determine the source of most
of the messes and figure out ways to thwart them before they occur.

Let's break it down by age.

Babies and Their Stuff

Clothes and bottles and diapers and wipes and teething rings and
bouncy seats and cribs and changing tables and strollers and high chairs
and infant-sized bathtubs and stuffed animals and pacifiers and wind-up
swings and baby monitors and...

And who knew that babies came with so much *stuff*?

Dealing with the baby is often a piece of cake; it's dealing with
baby accessories that can be quite the challenge. Where on earth are
you going to put it all?

First, designate a place for the larger items. If you don't create and
use a special place for the stroller, for example, then it will migrate from
the hall to the trunk of the car to a dusty corner of the garage, and
you'll never be able to find it when you need it.

Store like items with like: keep pacifiers in a plastic container in a
kitchen drawer, for example, and store bottles in one specific drawer or
cabinet. Otherwise they will end up all over the house.

Most of the messes babies make usually, unfortunately, involve disgusting bodily functions for which you will need to be adequately pre-

pared. Make sure you keep adequate supplies of diapers, wipes, and spit-up rags on hand. Running low on these types of supplies is courting disaster.

When my children were babies, the biggest offenders I ran across in the battle to keep my home straight and clean weren't so much wayward objects, but offensive *smells*. What's the point in having a spotlessly clean home if it smells like a sewer?

The answer lies in adequately containing the smells, then removing the offending object—usually poopy diapers—as quickly as possible. Use small plastic garbage bags—stored well out of baby's reach—to first seal the diaper. Then put the sealed bag in a Diaper Genie or other type of diaper-containment device. Empty the trash in the baby's room very frequently. Another option is to put the dirty diaper in a plastic bag, then take the bag straight to an outdoor trash can.

Cloth diapers are another option: if you choose to use a diaper service, they typically come once a week to remove the dirty diapers and leave fresh ones, and they provide fresheners to put in the dirty-diaper container, to keep offensive odors at bay. If you want to minimize diapering, keep in mind that babies who use cloth diapers typically toilet train a full 10-12 months sooner than their disposable-diaper-clad contemporaries, which is due to the fact that disposable diapers are so effective in removing liquid that it takes longer for babies to make the mental connection between the "need to go" and the uncomfortable sensation of wetness that is required for toileting. (For more information about using cloth diapers, visit www.DiaperNet.com.)

Orange- or citrus-scented air fresheners work particularly well in babies' rooms, by the way. Keep diaper-changing supplies in one or two centrally located locations, and always change the baby's diapers there, so you don't end up with diaper-changing supplies strewn all over the house.

Another room that tends to overflow with baby things is the bathroom. Supplies for bathing baby often include a special infant-sized tub, specially formulated soap and shampoo, and scads of baby bath toys.

To keep the mess contained, store it all in the baby's bathtub and keep it in the bottom of the shower when not in use. It's all out of sight and the mess will be contained.

For infants, or those who are not yet able to crawl, you can use a low basket in the living room or another central location to contain their toys. Spread a blanket on the floor and surround the baby with toys from the basket. Once playtime is over, toss the toys back into the basket, fold the blanket, and you're done.

Infants who are mobile present another set of housekeeping challenges, but perhaps the best way to contain the mess is to allow the baby to eat or drink in the kitchen *only*. Crumbs and leaky "sippy" cups can trash your décor in no time. To further simplify things, only offer food or drink to the baby when he or she is firmly strapped into the high chair (unless you're nursing, of course, but in that case there is no mess, so it's not an issue).

Baby toys can still be kept in a basket, but now you may want to stash a few baskets around the house in strategically located positions. Keep one in the kitchen, one in the family room, and one in the baby's room. Pick up the toys at regular intervals—during baby's naptime and before bed, at the very least. Losing control of the clutter at this stage leads to chaos in just a few short months, once babies become toddlers.

Finally, keep in mind that the marketing machine around anything remotely related to babies is powerful. The manufacturers that make all those precious, teensy clothes and "must-have" educational toys know that their window of opportunity is short, so they'll stop at nothing when it comes to trying to convince new parents to buy their wares.

Before you buy, take a step back and analyze the item you are contemplating purchasing. I once bought a CD of classical music for babies (for $14.95), only to discover when I got home that I had an almost identical version that I found in a bargain bin somewhere for $3.99.

Other items you may want to reconsider buying include large playthings that are only good for six to twelve months. Baby gyms are great, but they are expensive, their use is short-lived, and they take up a lot of room to store. Maybe you can suspend a few brightly colored toys above baby's play area instead and get the same effect (plus you can rotate the toys, so baby won't get bored).

Infant clothes, shoes, hats, hair bows, and headbands seem harmless enough when you're only looking at one or two outfits. The trouble starts when there are fifteen outfits, which the baby will outgrow in approximately three months, so a whole new wardrobe will be needed—which will also fit for approximately three months. The storage of all these outgrown clothes quickly becomes an issue for many families.

Another factor to consider is that baby clothes go through a lot of abuse. Most solid-colored outfits look good for one or two wearings but then succumb to the assault of dribbles, drool, and unmentionable organic substances. The end result is lots of stained but otherwise perfectly good infant clothes; they're too good to throw away but too stained to wear.

You can thwart a lot of these storage issues by (1) buying fewer items, and (2) selecting items that hide stains. If you are torn between selecting a flower-print tee or a solid field of pink or white, opt for the print every time.

Another tip: buy the basics at a discount store such as Target. It's much easier to get rid of a stained infant T-shirt that cost three dollars than an Egyptian cotton number from Neiman Marcus.

TIP: *Removing Baby Formula Stains*

Baby formula stains are notoriously difficult to remove. Instead of using expensive cleaners, try this trick: soak the stain first in isopropyl alcohol, then apply a regular stain remover. Let sit five minutes, then launder as usual.

Toddler Tips

This is perhaps the messiest stage of childhood. Toddlers are driven by an insatiable need to climb, feel, taste, touch, and explore their surroundings, but they are still too young to help pick things up in any meaningful way. This translates into a pint-sized house-wrecker with no sense of cleanliness or order. Thank goodness, this stage doesn't last long, but while you're in the thick of it time moves very s-l-o-w-l-y, so here are some tips to help you keep your sanity.

✦ Try to contain the mess by designating one or two rooms as play areas, then keeping other rooms off limits. In our house we allowed playing in the family room, kids' bedrooms, and the playroom. The master bedroom, dining room, and living room were off limits.

✦ Help kids pick up their clothes and toys at the end of the day. They are too young to do it by themselves, but by doing it with them you teach them to recognize and appreciate a sense of order, which they will learn to feel comfortable with and will eventually adopt themselves.

✦ Provide easy-to-reach storage containers for toys, such as baskets and bins. Clear plastic storage bins keep items from disappearing into the bottom, never to be seen again.

✦ Store toys with small pieces (such as pretend food, beads and jewelry, toy cars, or doll accessories) in clear, stackable storage boxes.

✦ Store board game pieces and puzzle pieces in small zip-lock bags inside the box. The pieces will stay contained and aren't as likely to slip through a torn corner of the box.

✦ Toddlers love to make arts and crafts, so keep supplies handy and contained in a large plastic storage bin. Fill the bin with construction paper, glue, glitter, cotton balls, craft sticks, stickers…whatever sounds like fun. But make sure that *everything* that goes into the box is washable and water-soluble. Another tip: store washable markers in a large zip-lock bag. The markers are easy to see, and if a top comes off of one or two markers they are less likely to dry out in the sealed plastic bag—or bleed ink onto other materials or toys.

✦ Designate an area for arts and crafts that is over an easy-to-clean floor. If the kids are painting or using glue or some other potentially disastrous substance, tape plastic garbage bags beneath the table and chairs.

✦ Teach kids to *always* use a plastic place mat at the kitchen table, whether they are eating, drinking, or working on a craft project.

✦ Kill two birds with one stone: for messy meals or projects, have the kids wear an old T-shirt that completely covers their clothes, or have them take off their shirts altogether. If they get paint or glue on their bodies, have them take a bath once the craft project is through. Or, if it's warm enough outside, send them outside to play in the sprinkler. You'll water your grass and get the kids relatively clean at the same time, plus they'll be out of the house while you clean up the craft mess.

✦ Make life easy on yourself and help kids adjust to a regular schedule. Kids thrive on structure. Letting kids get up when they want, go to bed too late, eat whenever, and watch television all day long isn't doing them any favors. Put kids to bed when you still have some energy, so you'll have some quiet, quality time to yourself at the end of every day.

✦ Make it easy for toddlers to help keep things orderly. Hang hooks that they can reach in their room, bathroom, and in the hall closet. Give them a place to put their toys, shoes, and books.

✦ Make the most of toddlers' desire to imitate everything they see you do. You can give a toddler a damp rag and have him help you dust furniture, or give him a toddler-sized broom and let him "help" you sweep. Other jobs toddlers can do include helping put (unbreakable) groceries in the pantry, or cleaning glass and windows. Look for ways to help them participate and be involved.

TIP: *Removing Marks on Walls*

To remove crayon marks from walls, rub the marks gently with a damp sponge and Colgate toothpaste. Marks made by pens, pencils, or scuff marks can be removed by gently rubbing with a dry cloth moistened with rubbing alcohol.

Occasionally a young, budding artist will stumble upon a permanent marker. For wall art of this variety, repainting the area is often the only effective solution. To make this an easy fix, when you paint a room put a small amount of paint in an airtight container that can be easily opened, such as a camera film canister or baby food jar. If the container is opaque, put a dab of paint on the top of the lid so you can easily tell what color is inside. Use the extra paint for emergency touch-ups.

To prevent permanent-marker mishaps in the future, do yourself a big favor: if you have young children and permanent markers anywhere in your house, put this book down right this second and go put the markers up in a very high, impossible-for-kids-to-reach location. This is important. Trust me.

KIDS' TOYS CLUTTERING THE TUB? TRY THIS

Nothing clutters an otherwise clean bathroom like the presence of children's bathtub toys. To keep the chaos contained, use a milk crate to stash the toys. Store the crate in the tub, where the water can run out the bottom and down the drain. Some stores and catalogs also sell mesh toy bags designed specifically for storing bathtub toys. Have the kids put their toys in the milk crate or mesh bag *before* they get out of the tub.

If the toys fill with water and then turn green and slimy on the inside, fill a plastic bowl with household bleach, squeeze the old yucky water out of the toys, submerge them in the bleach one by one, squeeze them, then allow them to suck in bleach. Let the toys sit, filled with bleach, overnight. Squeeze out the bleach, and the toys will be clean. (Be sure to wear rubber gloves.)

Once a month or so, cull through the bathtub toys and toss items that are worn, broken, faded, or have missing pieces. You can either enlist the kids to help, which will help them develop the difficult-to-master ability to throw things away, or you can do it when they are not in the room. What you want to avoid is sifting through their toys when they are in the room—or, worse, in the bathtub. If they aren't actively helping you, then your culling through their toys will be seen as an active attack on their playthings.

When you buy new toys for the bathtub, consider the cleanability factor first. Solid rubber toys that don't hold water stay the cleanest. Items such as plastic cups and measuring spoons encourage creative water play and are also very easy to clean—just pop them in the dishwasher once in a while.

ORGANIZING TODDLERS' CLOSETS AND TOYS

Children's wardrobes become a bit more manageable as they get older. Now you may get six months to a year or more out of an outfit, which means fewer clothes to buy and keep track of.

Now is the time to begin teaching kids to care for their own clothes. Low drawers and rods in the closet can make this much easier for tots, but remember that, until they are three or four, most kids are too young to do this fully by themselves. They need lots of help and instruction, but toddlers love to feel as though they are helping and contributing in some way. A toddler probably won't have the manual dexterity to hang his clothes on a hanger, but if you do that for him then he can put the hanger on the rod in the closet.

A small round laundry basket in the floor of the closet is a great place to store toddler shoes. They are contained, you can see through the basket to find mates, and children love rooting through the basket to find their shoes for the day. You can use another basket for dirty clothes, if you don't have a separate hamper.

Toys at this stage may begin to fall into categories. Designate a separate bin or crate for dolls, cars, balls, or trucks. The idea is to begin teaching your child to get things organized. An added benefit is that he will always know where to go to retrieve a certain toy.

Try to use containers that roughly approximate the shape of the toys that are stored there. For example, use a milk crate to store Barbies. The rectangular shape works well for storing the leggy dolls. Smooth the dolls' hair and clothes and lay them neatly in the crate, so they don't become mangled and disheveled. A compartmentalized storage box is great for storing Matchbox cars.

Making it easy for toddlers to help, to begin seeing their room and their clothes and their toys as something they can help keep neat and clean, is like laying a foundation. This is the beginning of teaching your child that things need to be taken care of. This doesn't happen overnight; it takes years before a child assumes the job entirely on his own, but the earlier you start the lessons, the sooner the results of your efforts begin to show.

Mother's Helper (4 to 8)

Things begin to get easier once kids hit this age range. In many cases they really *want* to help keep things straight. Helping them develop an awareness of what needs to be done is the task at hand.

At this age kids still need help when it comes to straightening and cleaning, although by the time they reach the older end of the spectrum, around age seven or eight, many kids are able to take on additional responsibilities.

Kids this age have a great eye for detail. If you give them a damp rag and ask them to dust the kitchen table, odds are good that they'll dust the table top, then you'll find them underneath the table, polishing the table legs as well.

Cleaning isn't a skill that children come by naturally (mine didn't, anyway). They need to be taught. Approaching the tasks, then, of straightening a bedroom or cleaning a bathroom can become an educational experience. Another thing: Kids don't naturally think of housework as drudgery. If you frame it right—at this age, in particular—young kids will enjoy pitching in to help.

Here are some ways you can entice young kids to help out around the house:

✦ Make it a game. "Whoever straightens their room first gets a popsicle!"

✦ Give them a hand. Kids will think it's a lot more fun if you are right there with them, pitching in to help.

✦ Put on some dance music. Spin a CD that makes you all want to boogie as you clean.

✦ Use a reward system of stickers or a special dessert after special cleaning accomplishments have been made. Or, put a prize at the finish line. "When we finish straightening the playroom we can all go outside and play!"

✦ Allow them the pride of accomplishment. Never let a child see you redoing the task they've just "finished." Once your child has completed a task, resist the temptation to straighten or polish something your child may have missed. Reward them instead with oohs and ahhs of admiration. Their sense of pride in their accomplishment is worth far more than a perfectly dusted table or streak-free window.

✦ Give a young child age-appropriate, enjoyable tasks that naturally suit his or her abilities and interests. A child who loves animals, for example, can be taught to feed the pets or clean the hamster cage. A child who loves to be outside can help weed a flower bed or water plants. And, although your knees may groan at the idea, these agile little monkeys love to get down on the floor and dust the chairs and legs of kitchen and dining room tables.

✦ Help kids learn to accomplish more difficult tasks, such as washing dishes, by having them practice with unbreakables first.

✦ If a child has trouble reaching the sink, give them a chair or a step-stool to stand on.

✦ You can facilitate young kids' independence by making it easy for them to reach their own plates, cups, and flatware.

✦ Teach kids to leave a room the way they found it: drawers should be shut and toys picked up before moving on to another room.

✦ Help kids determine a place for each of their possessions. Give them child-sized containers to store things in.

✦ Hang lots of hooks at their level so they can keep coats, backpacks, and wet towels off the floor.

SETTING THE COURSE

It is unrealistic to expect your child to automatically know how to clean something, even if they've seen you do it several times. One very effective way to help teach a child a task is to type up and print out a worksheet for her or him to follow. (The child must be old enough to read for this to work.) Let's say, for example, that you are teaching your child to clean his room. Type up a worksheet that looks something like this:

How to Clean Your Room

1. Pick up any trash on the floor, on your desk, or under your bed, and throw it in the waste basket.

2. Pick up dirty clothes that are on the floor, on the bed, over a chair, or anywhere else, and put them in a laundry hamper.

3. Fold or hang and then put away any clean clothes that are in the room but not where they belong.

4. Pick up shoes and put them in the closet neatly.

5. Pick up toys and put them where they belong. Pick up large toys first, and then move on to smaller toys.

6. Make your bed.

7. Use a barely damp rag to dust your desk, bookshelves, window sill, and any other dusty surfaces in the room.

8. Vacuum the floor.

9. Take a final look around your room and enjoy your handiwork!

GOT KIDS IN THE HOUSE?
10 STAIN-BUSTING TRICKS YOU SHOULD KNOW

1. Buy only light, clear drinks, such as apple juice, lemonade, and white cranberry juice. If you splurge on treats, buy vanilla cookies, or snacks coated with white chocolate or yogurt.

2. Train youngsters to keep food *in the kitchen*. Snacks that roam only spread the mess.

3. Provide a drawer or shelf for plastic drinking cups and melamine plates and bowls that the kids can reach.

4. Put a multi-hued, durable, relatively inexpensive rug under the kitchen table, which will hide crumbs and can be easily vacuumed clean.

5. Have a baby in a high chair? Keep a dropcloth underneath, to make cleaning up spills a breeze.

6. Teach kids to wipe up spills themselves. Keep a hand towel near the kitchen table so you'll be prepared when the inevitable occurs.

7. Have young children drink from plastic, spill-proof "sippy" cups. (These are also great for ailing adults. When someone isn't feeling well and wants to drink in bed or from a horizontal position on the couch, a sippy cup makes things much easier.)

8. Have children eat messy foods such as ice cream or popsicles outside. Weather permitting, you can hose them off when they're done, which they will think is great fun!

9. Keep a stash of baby wipes to clean up minor spills. These are also great for cleaning small hands and faces.

10. Remember that childhood is fleeting. An occasional stain will later serve to remind you of the days when the children were young.

Babysitter Know-How

If you have young children and make use of babysitters at all, then you know firsthand what a joy it is to come home to clean, happy, well-fed children and a well-kept home. You also probably know firsthand the agony of leaving a relatively clean home and returning a few hours later to a thoroughly trashed abode.

As the parents of two relatively young children, my husband and I use babysitters regularly. We are astounded by the different skills and abilities of the different babysitters we encounter. Some clearly have been well trained and are more than prepared to deal with running a house, even for just a few hours, while others seem completed unprepared to deal with the various messes that result from simply playing with little kids for a while, feeding them, and getting them ready for bed.

One sitter left the playroom looking like a toy bomb had been detonated. My own children had never left the room in such disarray. Toy boxes had been dumped, and pieces of games and puzzles lay strewn about the room. I wanted to cry.

Another sitter, a fine young girl that the children love dearly, seems to be physically incapable of shutting cabinet doors. When we come home the toys are picked up, the family room is straightened, but every single cabinet door in the kitchen is wide open. This kid is not passive-aggressive; she's not leaving the doors open to annoy us. She just hasn't been taught to shut cabinet doors.

If your goal is to outwit housework, and you use babysitters at all, then you can prevent many cleaning headaches by setting expectations high and asking sitters to not let the house fall into a state of complete disarray. I'm not advocating hiring a sitter based on his or her ability to clean, but I am suggesting that you spend a bit of time looking for someone who is competent to both watch and entertain your kids, and keep the house tidy, too.

'Tweens (9 to 12)

If you've got a 'tween on your hands, lucky you! This is a great age when kids are happy to pitch in and just need a bit of direction.

If your 'tween has largely lived a carefree life until this point without having to help out around this house, don't despair. It's not too late to instill in your child a sense of how and why it's important to help keep the house in order.

It may be a good idea to have a family meeting to talk about habits and methods around the house that are not working. Get their input. Find out what is important to them, what chores they don't mind doing, what it is they really hate.

I remember having a discussion with my mom when I was about 10. We were unloading the dishwasher together and she asked me what my favorite part of unloading the dishwasher was. "The big stuff," I replied. "I like putting up the pots and pans, because if I just put up one or two things then the dishwasher is already halfway unloaded!"

She was surprised. "I like putting up the flatware," she said. I wrinkled my nose in distaste. "Ick! That's the *worst* part," I replied. So, from then on, I did the big stuff and she put away the flatware.

Here are some jobs that are great for 'tweens:

✦ Fold and put away laundry.

✦ Walk the dog.

✦ Clean the kitchen.

✦ Wash windows.

✦ Cook simple meals with supervision.

✦ Change their own sheets.

✦ Iron clothes.

✦ Weed a flower bed.

✦ Dust and vacuum.

TIP: *The Ball Bin*

Specialty stores that cater to schools sell storage containers for balls that can make life much easier if you have balls scattered all over your house and yard. Both indoor and outdoor models are available. The outdoor models are on wheels, which means they can be carted around the yard, then wheeled into the garage for safe, dry storage. Check out www.WolverineSports.com.

Teenagers (13+)

Once kids hit the teen years, much of the foundation has been laid for how much and how well they help out around the house. By this time they have either learned how to pitch in and help, or they have learned that they really don't have to help out much at all.

Other factors come into play with teenagers, too. A blossoming need for privacy, pizza, and what may seem like an excessive need for sleep can leave your teen barricaded in their room, hibernating in conditions you wouldn't want the Health Department to see.

Fortunately for parents, there's another side of the coin. Teens can also be passionate about their social lives. They live for contact with other teenage aliens. It is this desperate need for social contact that parents can rely upon to motivate a reluctant teen. (I know this because this is how my parents motivated *me*.)

A teenager wants to use the car on Friday night? Great! Once his room is clean he is free to use the car! Or hang out at the mall with friends! Or whatever it is he wants to do…tie the desired behavior to the reward.

This may smack of bribery, but really it is a matter of trading what one person wants (your teen wants to use the car) for what another person wants (you want some help around the house). There is nothing unfair about this system.

As with younger children, keep a list of previously agreed-upon chores posted in a prominent spot, so your requests for help won't seem arbitrary or impulsive. And make sure that your teen understands the stakes before 7 P.M. on Friday. It's not fair to spring a long list of demands on a teenager who is itching to join a party at a friend's house that has already started.

Teenagers can do just about anything around the house that you can do, but take care not to burden them too heavily. Pressures from school and an active social life can leave teens feeling overwhelmed, so make sure their list of chores is realistic and that you both agree to them before the rules are posted.

The upshot is that willing teenagers can help out around the house *a lot*. If you give them a generous allowance (more about this shortly) in return, then this easily can be a win/win proposition.

Here are some things a teen can do:

✦ Cook dinner one or two nights a week.

✦ Clean up after dinner.

✦ Mow the grass.

✦ Wash the car.

✦ Vacuum, dust, and straighten common living areas.

✦ Clean their own room thoroughly.

✦ Clean their own bathroom.

✦ Polish silver.

✦ Collect the trash and take it outside.

Motivating Kids to Help

As children get older they usually lose a bit of their eagerness to pitch in and help out around the house. Many parents find that they are more successful when they *encourage* the kids to help, as opposed to browbeating them with dark insinuations and threats.

You can try this: *"Don't you dare leave this room in a mess!"*

Or this: *"Sweetie, would you please fold that blanket and take your glass to the kitchen when this show is over?"*

Which request would *you* respond better to?

Another tactic is to have a few set chores for which each family member is responsible. A four-year-old can toss toys into a basket every night before going to bed; an eight-year-old can take drinking glasses to the kitchen. Once the kids get into a familiar routine, helping keep the house straight will become a habit.

The key here is consistency. If you ask a child to help once a month, then the request is likely to seem unusual and unnecessary.

Why should I have to do it today? I don't usually do that! Someone else does that! This is the child's reasoning. Something they are trained to do every day feels more natural, like brushing their teeth.

Selling your family members on the worthiness of the goal of having a cleaner, more organized home is vital to outwitting housework. You've got to convince them that having a clean house is well worth the extra time and energy it takes, but how?

One way to motivate kids to help out around the house is to appeal to their sense of reason. Talk it out. How many people live in your house? Two? Three? Four? Six? It takes that many people to get your house dirty; it should take more than one to keep it clean. Children have an innate sense of fairness and will often respond to rational explanation.

Probably the most effective way to enlist the troops is to take the drudgery out of cleaning. Make it *fun*, something you pitch in and do together. *Games* are a lot more enjoyable than *chores*. Put on funky dance music so you can groove together as you clean. Young children can be challenged to have a dusting race, or set a timer and see how many shelves your child can dust in three minutes *("Ready? Set? Go!")*. Or, hide a few coins throughout the house so they can look for hidden pennies as they clean. Older kids can be motivated to pitch in by offering a reward once chores are done: a family game, pizza night, going out to see a movie, or monetary reward can all be used to effectively motivate kids to pitch in and help.

Another way to encourage family members to get into the habit of keeping things tidy is to spend some time every evening with each of your kids in their rooms, helping them get things in order. Help them put things where they belong; keep them from seeking shortcuts by stuffing things under the bed or into the closet. (I know I mentioned this earlier, but it bears repeating: Most kids—even teens—really appreciate having an adult help them keep things in order. Not only does the room get straightened, but it's a great way to spend a bit of relaxed time together, working toward a common goal.)

As you help your family develop good habits in the clean-home department, be on the lookout for strategies that work and strategies that aren't so effective. Notice the circumstances that cause your kids to pitch in good-naturedly, and also notice what makes them groan. By monitoring their responses you can tailor your approach.

Many families find the battle to keep kids' rooms neat to be a never-ending source of tension and conflict. You want the room to look presentable, while kids have an innate desire to create and then cocoon in a space of their making. They don't care how it looks to the outside world (or to adults, anyway). They just want the space to be their own.

In these instances a compromise may be the solution. Have the kids clean their rooms once a week, then shut the door in between cleanings. In this way fire hazards and insect infestations are avoided, but the kids get to keep a sense of ownership over "their space."

Finally, help family members make the mental connection that they stand to benefit when things are neat and clean. Say things like this: "Man, your rooms look great! Since we don't have much cleaning to do, let's celebrate by going out for ice cream!" Or, try this on your spouse or significant other: "Thanks so much for cleaning up the kitchen after dinner. Now we have time to cuddle up on the couch and watch a movie together."

TIP: A Quick Fix for Messy Rooms

For kids whose rooms tend to be messy—okay, revolting pigpens—one very effective approach is to calmly point out that piles of clothes on the floor attract spiders and, in some areas, scorpions, while leftover food, wrappers, and containers attract ants and roaches. The *ick* factor is often enough to motivate even very messy kids to keep their clothes off the floor.

Should You Pay Your Kids to Help with Housework?

Experts caution that many children are not taught fiscal responsibility—not at an early age, and, in many cases, not at all. While the argument can be made that kids should pitch in and help out with chores without being paid because they live in the house, too, many parents (okay, me) find that this is an unrealistic approach.

While there are definitely some things that I expect my kids to help out with just by virtue of the fact that *we're all in this together* and *they live in this house, too*, I have found that giving them the incentive of an allowance tied to an agreed-upon set of chores is a more effective way to solicit their help.

In addition to establishing good habits, such as picking up after themselves and making their beds every morning, setting up an allowance system and encouraging children to save for toys or books they want is a good way to introduce them to sound financial principles.

How much should your child's allowance be? A good rule of thumb is to pay a child the dollar amount of their age every week. So, an eight-year-old gets eight dollars a week. In our house we tie performance to the allowance: if chores are only done halfway, then the allowance amount is prorated to reflect the amount of work that was actually done. Keeping track of your child's chores is easy if you introduce a simple, one-page chart and keep it in an accessible place, like on the refrigerator, so your child will be reminded of the chores on their list without you having to remind or nag.

Use a different chart for each child, and remember that children of different ages have different skills and abilities, so make their chores age-appropriate.

Some families find that keeping track of chores on a week-to-week basis just doesn't work for them. They forget about the system or fail to use it systematically, so the plan doesn't work. These families may find it easier to perform and pay on a daily basis. A child who makes his bed, straightens his room, helps with dishes after dinner, and feeds the dog—or whatever his chores may be—gets a dollar (or 50 cents, or whatever you agree upon in advance) at the end of the day. This is a great system for those who tend to "fall off the wagon" when it comes to teaching their kids about helping out around the house. It's easy to reestablish this system quickly if it falls by the wayside, and the kids are motivated and reinforced by the instant gratification of being paid on the same day that the tasks are performed.

Chapter Ten

PETS, VEHICLES, AND OTHER MOBILE MESSES

Not all areas of disarray are easily categorized. In this chapter we will take a look at a few specific areas of cleaning challenges and examine ways to thwart them.

Cats and Dogs and Birds, Oh My!

Pets are wonderful family additions that provide a whole host of clean-ing, *ahem,* challenges. Keep in mind that how much you love your pet and how much you want to remove the signs of their presence in your home are not related!

Removing the disgusting by-products of a pet who has thrown up, urinated, or defecated in your lovely abode are key aspects of dealing with pets. If you're going to have them in the house, you need to find an effective way to promptly deal with their messes.

A pet who routinely has "accidents" in your home requires more ac-tion than a pet who merely is left inside too long and can't hold it any longer. Regular accidents amount to an animal staking his claim and marking territory, or dealing with anxiety issues over being left alone.

Cats who spray are perhaps the worst, or most detectable, of pet problems in the home. A cat who sprays may need to be neutered or contained in a room without carpet or upholstered furniture when you're not home, and there are products that can be applied to carpet and furniture to discourage this type of behavior. Talk to your vet about your options for training a cat or dog who is territorially marking carpet or furniture in your house.

So, your pet has had an accident. Here's how you clean it up:

1. Remove any solid waste with a wad of paper towels. Here's a great technique: put your hand inside a plastic grocery bag, then pick up the paper towels with the bagged hand, pick up the waste, then turn the bag inside out, and the waste will be neatly con-tained. Be careful to lift it straight off the carpet or rug, so you don't make things any worse.

2. If the pet has urinated on carpet, use a clean, white towel and a rubber-soled shoe, then stand on the towel, turning it frequently, until you can't soak up any more at all—not another drop.

3. Next, take a white rag, get it wet, then add a drop or two of dish-washing liquid. Use the rag to lightly scrub the soiled carpet until

there is nothing visible remaining. Keep turning the rag so you're using a clean part frequently.

4. Finish with a stain- and odor-removing solution (see box).

Shameless Product Endorsement #2:

Woolite Pet Stain Carpet & Upholstery Cleaner

Here we go, one more reason to trust Woolite. This stuff is amazing. "Safely cleans tough pet stains" is what the label promises, and darned if this product doesn't deliver. It's the best product I've found for eliminating residual odor from pet urine stains, but, as with all unwanted substances on carpet, you'll get the best results if you can get to the stain immediately after it occurs.

Some product specialists caution against using ammonia-based products to deal with pet urine; if the pet is marking territory, then the ammonia in the product can encourage repeated marking. However, for true pet *accidents* and a lingering smell that other products aren't able to remove, I have found that a weakened solution of an ammonia-based cleaner, such as Mr. Clean or Pine-Sol, can be very effective in neutralizing any residual odor. Be sure to test carpet or upholstery in an inconspicuous spot first to make sure the product won't stain.

Fur and Feathers Running Amok

Unfortunately, "accidents" aren't the only signs that pets live in a home. Potentially more insidious are the hair, fur, and feathers that most pets leave in their wake.

Regular grooming of pets with long hair or who tend to shed is the first, best course of action you can take to keep your home relatively free of fur. A good brushing removes dirt and shedding fur, stimulates your pet's skin and coat, reduces hairballs, and makes for a happier, more contented pet. Make it a habit to brush your dog or cat once a day, even if only for a few minutes. (This is a great job for kids, too, if your pet will tolerate it.)

The next best way to contain loose pet fur is to have your pet sleep in a designated area. A soft, fluffy bed for a dog or a cushy folded blanket in a comfortable nook for a cat can keep the shedding fur somewhat contained.

If you're serious about reducing the amount of visible fur in your home, invest in a carpet or in area rugs that closely approximate the color of your pet's fur. (How I ended up with a *black* cat and a *white* dog is a lengthy, boring story, but the end result is that camouflage décor is not an option in my house. Try to avoid this sorry state of affairs.)

In the summer, when pet shedding is most problematic, have pets with long coats trimmed or even shaved by a professional groomer. Your pet will look a bit odd, but he'll feel better without a heavy coat during the hot summer months, and your house will stay much cleaner.

TIP: *How to Have a Stink-Free Litter Box*

If your cat uses a litter box and keeping the stinky thing clean is a job you detest, then look for disposable, pre-filled cat litter trays, which are carried by some grocery store chains and pet-supply stores. The trays cost a bit more than the traditional method—about $2.50 for a tray that lasts a week—but the payoff is significant: you'll never have to clean the cat box again.

These lightweight plastic trays come filled with litter, then covered with paper. Tear the paper off, and the tray is ready to go. After a week or so, slide the whole thing into a plastic bag and throw it away. (I find that the tray lasts even longer if I add several cups of absorbent, scented litter to the tray when I first set it out.)

Keep the tray outside, in the garage or on a patio, if at
all possible. You may need to install a kitty door so your cat
can go back and forth, but the mess and the smell will be
removed from your home and will be much better ventilated.

FEATHERED FRIENDS

We've covered dogs and cats, but what about birds?

Although pet birds can add a great deal of beauty, music, and entertainment to your home, man, do they ever make a mess.

Before you invest in a feathered friend, consider the beauty and
practicality of fostering a bird-friendly environment in the area *outside*
your home, in your yard, patio, or garden. A consistently stocked bird
feeder will attract a wide variety of birds to an area where you can see
and hear them, but you won't have to clean up after them.

What if it's too late and you already have a pet bird? There are two
primary areas to keep the birdcage away from if you want to minimize
the mess: over carpet, and anywhere near an area where you eat.

The real mess from keeping birds is almost invisible to the naked
eye: lots of fine dust that includes waste particles and mites drifts
around the area surrounding a birdcage. Hang the cage over a solid-
surface floor that can be easily and routinely damp-mopped, and keep
lots of premoistened towelettes on hand so you can quickly swipe up
the inevitable dust.

If you have a particularly messy bird who flings bird seed and empty
seed hulls around his cage with reckless abandon, keep a handi-vac
plugged in near the cage so you can remove the debris quickly and easily.
You may also need to switch to a cage that has enclosed sides more than
halfway up the side of the cage, which helps contain a lot of the mess. Alternatively, you can set the cage into an open, clear-sided storage container, but make sure the bird has at least one perch that enables it to see

above and beyond the sides of the box. The container will hold the mess
that spills beyond the confines of the cage.

Guerrilla Gerbils

One family had a problem with the family's two gerbils, who bur-
rowed and dug into the fluffy filler that lined their cage until the
messy material covered the desk and floor surrounding the cage—
every day. "The mess was driving me crazy," said the mother, "but I
wanted to keep the cage accessible since the kids played with the
gerbils all the time. A self-contained cage would have kept them from
being able to play with the pets." The solution? "I set the entire cage
inside the bottom half of a large, clear-plastic storage container. The
kids could easily reach over the sides to play with the gerbils, and the
fluff the gerbils kicked out of the cage was neatly contained."

TIP: *It's a Dirty Job...*

...so make sure to keep a box of disposable rubber gloves
handy.

For particularly nasty jobs, such as emptying kitty's litter
box or cleaning out a bird cage, pop on a disposable pair
of latex gloves—the kind health care professionals wear.
You can buy them at drug and grocery stores, and the
cost is minimal—just pennies a pair. These are also useful
for more mundane tasks, such as mixing meatloaf or
polishing silver.

Tips for Keeping Your Car a Clean Machine

Even if you manage to keep your house relatively clean and straight, keeping your car clean can be an almost insurmountable challenge. Commuters—those highly caffeinated rush-hour cowboys who comprise the bulk of traffic jams—clog our freeways and side streets to the point where many of us live a large part of our lives in the car, stuck in traffic.

Some of us live in the suburbs, where we can enjoy a bit of space and a slower pace of life, only to jump into the commuting throng to get to a more centrally located workplace during the work week. Others join the roadway masses as they schlep children and teens from one activity to another.

Our vehicles don't only transport us; they take all our stuff along for the ride, too. This home-away-from-home tends to accumulate junk just like our real home. Maps and coffee mugs are just the beginning: CDs, fast-food wrappers and bags, soda cans, ash trays that need to be emptied, book bags, toys, clothes en route to and from the dry cleaners, and a wide variety of miscellaneous items such as runaway shoes, jackets, sports equipment, items purchased from stores, items put in the car to *return* to the store…. All of this can quickly coalesce into an unmanageable avalanche of stuff unless you have a plan.

QUICK 5: HOW TO CLEAN YOUR VEHICLE IN A HURRY

1. Purchase gasoline at a station with a brushless car wash. Let the automatic car wash do the hard work.

2. Throw away all trash.

3. Use a handi-vac to quickly vacuum up dirt and debris.

4. Use a disposable quick wipe to clean the interior of the car.

5. Give the windows a quick shine with glass cleaner.

30 Ways to Keep Your Vehicle Looking Great

1. If you have a garage or carport, keep a trash can in close proximity to the place where you park your car. When you arrive home, make it a habit to quickly scavenge for trash in the car and toss it into the can. Teach your kids to do the same.

2. Never pass a trash can without feeding it something! When you go to work or run errands, look for sidewalk trash cans as you park and deposit any trash from the car. Make it a habit to throw away trash when you stop for gas. The habit of frequently looking for trash in your car to throw away will keep it free of rubbish.

3. Kids are notorious car trashers. Keep a small plastic storage container in the car where kids can stash their travel toys, notebooks, and rinky-dink McToys. Keep a small hand towel in the car to quickly deal with the inevitable spills.

4. Keep a small, round laundry basket in the back seat or in the trunk where you can contain dirty clothes that are on their way to the dry cleaners.

5. Invest in a portable CD case to keep your music CDs tidy and organized.

6. If your trunk tends to attract an unorganized hodgepodge of items, use a trunk organizer—available in auto stores—to keep things straight.

7. Keep a travel-sized container of handi-wipes in the glove box and use them to quickly wipe off dusty interior surfaces of your car, such as the dashboard, when you're stuck in traffic. (You can save a few dollars by storing a few wipes from home in a zip-lock bag and foregoing the pricey travel-sized container. The zip-lock saves space, too.)

8. Does your car smell musty? You can buy an auto deodorizer to keep things smelling fresh, or you can tuck a sachet into an unobtrusive pocket and freshen it occasionally with a few drops of es-

sential oil. (I combine the two methods and use essential oil to refresh a store-bought auto deodorizer, which I keep tucked away in a well-ventilated mesh pocket in the back seat.)

9. Use regular carpet cleaner to remove spills and stains from the carpet in your car.

10. When cleaning the carpet in your vehicle, remember that the carpet is backed by steel, which will rust. Don't get the carpet too wet, and thoroughly blot up any spills immediately.

11. Keep things that you store in the car pint-sized. Unless you have a raging head cold, keep boxes of tissues at home, not in the car. A small travel-size pack in the glove box is all you need.

12. Encourage thirsty passengers to drink only clear liquids such as water or Sprite. Unless the interior upholstery in your car is ruby red, Hawaiian Punch is a big no-no.

13. Use quick wipes to remove the smell of gasoline from your hands after filling the tank.

14. A mixture of baking soda and water will remove automotive grease from your hands.

15. Keep a bag of scented, non-clumping kitty litter in the trunk of your car, which you can use for traction if you get stuck in mud or snow. In the meantime, the scented litter will keep the trunk interior smelling fresh.

16. Clean nooks and crannies inside your car with a sponge-tipped paintbrush or Q-Tip soaked in an all-purpose cleanser.

17. Rub a piece of waxed paper up and down your automatic retracting radio antenna to keep it gliding smoothly.

18. The easiest way to clean corroded battery terminals is to pour carbonated soda over the gunk and let it bubble away the corrosion.

19. Laundry pre-wash liquid removes tar from automotive paint.

20. Never use dishwashing detergent to wash your car; it dissolves wax and can damage the paint's finish. Use specially formulated car-wash liquid instead.

21. Prevent rust on your car's undercarriage by putting a lawn sprinkler under your car and turning it on full blast. Move the sprinkler so that it washes dirt, salt, and grime from all areas.

22. Buy a small tube of matching paint from your auto dealer to touch up small chips in your car's finish. Or, apply a small dot of clear fingernail polish to paint chips in your car's finish to prevent rust.

23. A blackboard eraser can be used to wipe condensation off the interior of your windshield.

24. To prevent streaking, don't wash your car in the sun.

25. Replace worn floor mats, which are available from the dealer, auto parts stores, and retailers such as Target, to quickly and inexpensively improve the appearance of your car's interior.

26. Wet, wash, and then rinse one section of the vehicle at a time so soap suds don't dry on the paint.

27. Clean bird droppings off of your vehicle as soon as you notice them; the high acid content will corrode paint quickly.

28. Coca-Cola poured on a piece of crumpled aluminum foil will clean rust off a metal bumper.

29. Clean headlights and chrome with a mixture of baking soda and water.

30. Use a wet nylon sponge and baking soda to remove dead bugs from the grill and windshield.

TIP: *Gadgets That Help Keep Your Car Clean*

Many drivers spend over an hour a day in the car, which can make this small space a home-away-from-home. If you routinely cart kids or pets around, consider investing in a NeatSeat, a machine-washable, suede-like car-seat protector that slides over your car seat like a slipcover ($149.99, www.BestFriendsCompany.net).

To keep things organized, Car Hanger Hooks, a 12-inch bar that attaches to the back of a headrest, has four hooks and is great for stashing things like umbrellas, plastic grocery bags, and even purses (from Get Organized, $9.98).

To clean windows and mirrors fast, keep a travel pack of window cleaner wipes in your car's glove compartment ($9.95, www.GriotsGarage.com, 800-345-5789).

Another great product from Griot's for spot-cleaning your car's painted surfaces: Speed Shine Wipes. These soft towelettes easily remove dust, grease, and messy bird hits quickly and easily (the Travel Pack is $9.95, www.GriotsGarage.com).

Chapter Eleven

L. Heidorn

THE GREAT OUTDOORS

Outwitting housework isn't just an indoor task. That's the bad news. The good news is that figuring out a way to keep your yard and the exterior of your house clean and free of debris and clutter is guaranteed to produce results. You'll please yourself, your family, and the neighbors; add to the aesthetic appeal of your home; and probably increase your property value, too.

Perennially Pleasing

Even if you love to garden and work in the yard, having a well-kept yard takes a lot of time and energy. Is it possible to cut corners and still have a good-looking yard? Can you have the benefits without the work?

Absolutely.

There's one word you should know if you want to minimize the time you spend in your yard: *perennials*. Hardy perennials are robust plants that renew themselves and tend to spread from year to year. They usually hold their own against competition and fill spaces that may have previously needed weeding or mowing. Simply put, the more perennials you have, the less yard work you'll have to do. This is not to say that your perennials won't need tending; mature plants periodically need dividing, feeding, weeding, deadheading, and mulching. But a perennial garden, once established, takes far less maintenance than a bed of annuals or grass.

Because you will be living with the results for a long time, take care when choosing perennials. Consult a local landscape nursery for recommendations, and take advantage of the endless supply of landscape guides that are available. Look for a guide that specializes in garden planning in your area, or zone, and watch out for non-native, invasive plants that can take over a garden before you turn around. (I once planted mint in a brick patio container, only to have the roots grow through the *bottom* of the planter and crop up outside the confines of the container!)

Conversely, the most labor-intensive fixture you can possibly have in your yard is also the most ubiquitous: grass. A lush, well-kept lawn requires staggering amounts of water, fertilizer, and weed killer, not to mention the time spent keeping it mowed and edged. If you want to minimize lawn care, carve out flower beds and fill the space with perennials, or plant lush fields of wildflowers or ground covers.

Flowing, gently curved flower beds are more natural-looking and are easier to maintain than their geometric counterparts. When determining where to make flower beds, lay out a water hose to help visualize the most aesthetically pleasing arrangement.

Ground covers such as English ivy, ajuga, monkeygrass, liriope, vinca, trailing juniper, or Asian jasmine are a nice way to fill in either flower beds or ground previously covered by grass. Ground covers help keep down weeds and shelter the roots of larger bushes and shrubs.

Using native plants is another strategy to keep your yard looking its best with a minimum amount of effort. Native plants are plants that thrive in your area naturally. They are acclimated to the weather and soil in your area and are resistant to the pests and diseases that may prey upon other, less robust plants that do not thrive in your area naturally. Some nurseries specialize in natives; ask a professional landscaper about plants that do well in your area, and keep an eye out in your neighborhood for plant varieties that thrive. Once natives get established, they will require very little if any upkeep.

Be Prepared

As with any other type of home maintenance, the job will go much more smoothly if you are physically and mentally prepared for the task at hand.

Before working in the yard, put on the right clothes. Gardening usually means getting down and dirty, so make sure your knees are covered. If you are allergic to any plants or weeds, wear a long-sleeved T-shirt. Wear a good-fitting pair of waterproof garden gloves to protect your hands and fingernails and keep them clean.

Nurseries and some catalogs sell thick foam mats that you can use as you move about the garden, weeding or planting, but a sturdy pair of knee pads works just as well, and they have the added benefit of going with you wherever you putter about, so you don't have to lug the mat all around the garden.

Finally, keep a small bucket with a handle nearby as you work. You can use it to move small tools around with you, and it makes a perfect container for the occasional pulled weed or bit of yard debris.

ALTERNATIVE PEST PATROL

Before you cave in to the temptation to nuke all garden pests to kingdom come with pesticides and harsh chemicals, consider these alternatives:

✦ Aphids can be manually washed off infested plants every three to four days, or a mild soapy wash can be used to keep the aphids at bay for longer stretches of time. Some plants such as parsley discourage aphids, as do spiders and ladybugs.

✦ Slugs can be treated with a commercially available iron phosphate compound such as WorryFree that is safe for children and pets; slugs stop eating as soon as they ingest the pellets, then they die a few days later. Be very careful with slug bait that contains metaldehyde; it can be very dangerous to children and pets.

✦ Light outdoor citronella candles or torches containing citronella oil a half hour before you go outside, or a half hour before dusk, to allow the scent to repel mosquitoes before they start biting.

✦ Consult a guide such as *Rodale's Encyclopedia of Insect and Plant Diseases,* or *Dead Snails Leave No Trails: Natural Pest Control for Home and Garden,* by Loren Nancarrow and Janet Hogan Taylor, for other ways to discourage pests naturally.

Zone Defense

If you have a large yard, it helps to mentally break the yard into zones. A yard of about an acre needs to be broken down into three or four zones, for example. A smaller yard can be broken into two: front and back. The idea is to break the job down into small, manageable jobs instead of having one huge, daunting task.

When the time to do yard work rolls around, focus on one zone at a time. Don't set out to "weed the yard." Set out to "weed the south side of the back yard." This makes the task much more accomplishable. Once you've finished that zone, you can either finish for the day or move on to a second zone. If you decide to call it a day, however, you won't be plagued by a sense of incompletion. Instead of failing to "weed the yard," instead you "successfully weeded one zone." The mental difference in this pattern of thinking is significant. It can keep you from becoming demoralized, which is key when the task at hand threatens to overwhelm.

Time-Saving Tips for a Healthy Lawn

Carefree lawn care begins, literally, at the roots. If your grass is healthy it will require less water, weed killer, and chemical fertilizer. Aerating and using organic fertilizers can help get your grass in tip-top shape.

Next, get a mulching lawn mower. The grass clippings on the lawn not only save you the trouble of disposing of them, but they return nitrogen to the soil so you can fertilize less often.

Finally, let your grass grow out a few inches before you cut it. The shaved-lawn look is passé, anyway. Longer grass shades the roots and retains moisture, which helps keep the grass healthy and resistant to drought and disease.

Hire a Teen

If you despise gardening and yard work, then you probably need to come to terms with the fact that you won't be winning "Yard of the Month" any time soon (unless you hire a landscaping company to take care of the job for you). Professional yard care can be pricey, but there is one very good yet frequently overlooked option: teenagers.

Find a young, energetic workhorse in or around your neighborhood with a little bit of time on his or her hands. Like babysitters, teenagers who work in your yard for you will probably need to be groomed a bit to suit your particular needs and desires. You'll need to tell them how high to cut the grass, maybe show them how to edge the grass, or how to pull weeds properly. But in the end the result will be well worth the trouble: you'll have a nice, kept lawn at a fraction of the price of a professional landscaper, and you'll be helping a teen at the same time. (An added benefit of this plan is that it employs teens during the summer, when they are out of school and have time available, and when—coincidentally—yard-maintenance needs are at a peak.)

TOP TIPS FOR THE GARDEN

✦ Paint or wrap (with plastic tape) the handles of your garden tools with bright, fluorescent colors to make them easy to spot as you work in the garden.

✦ Large vegetable gardens can quickly fill with weeds and be difficult to maintain. Consider raised-bed or planter gardening instead.

✦ Remember that the more showy and faster-growing a plant is, the messier it will be.

✦ When you plant (or transplant) something, toss a handful of bone meal, fertilizer, and slow-release water pellets into the hole first, to promote root formation and help the plant get established.

✦ During the summer months transplant or set in new plants in the evening and water them well, to give them a chance to adjust before the hot summer sun beats down.

✦ To help plants get off to a healthy start, plant them as soon as you get them home from the nursery.

✦ Plant ground cover in or heavily mulch the areas that are most plagued by weeds.

✦ Group thirsty plants together near your water source, to conserve both time and water.

Spring Cleaning 101

Cleaning up a yard after a full season of blowing leaves and rain, snow, sleet, and muck can be a daunting task. Many landscape companies offer Spring Specials where they'll bring in heavy-duty equipment and teams of gardeners for the task. While this can be a great way to get a head start on spring and summer yard maintenance, many homeowners prefer to do the job themselves.

Where to begin?

START WITH THE MOST VISIBLE PORTION OF YOUR YARD

Getting the most visible portion of your yard cleaned up first will give you an immediate sense of instant gratification, which will power you through the rest of the task.

GET THE BIG JOBS OUT OF THE WAY

Figure out the single biggest offenders in your yard and get those tasks over with. If weeds have run amok, hire a teenager or yard-care company to help, but get that job done and out of the way. If leaves have accumulated, rake them up and throw them away. Once the big offenders are gone, the task of getting your yard ready for spring won't seem nearly as daunting.

CONSULT A SPECIALIST

Unless you're an ace gardener, this is the time to seek the advice of a garden professional at a local nursery. You'll be there looking for plants and supplies anyway. Find out what your yard needs to help it recover from the winter and get ready for spring. You may need to fertilize or put down pre-emergent, which prevents weeds from sprouting once the weather warms up a bit; your local gardening expert will probably be thrilled to talk shop and let you know what you need to do next.

MAKE BASIC REPAIRS

Winter conditions can be tough on elements of your yard such as fences, paths and walkways, and even outdoor furniture. Once the thaw of spring arrives, take a survey around your yard and inspect for any damage that may have occurred. Look for broken fence posts, rotted wood, cracks in sidewalks, chips in brick-and-mortar paths, and outdoor furniture that needs to be resealed or repainted. Get these repairs taken care of before things get really busy with summer work and play.

JOIN FORCES WITH THE NEIGHBORS

If you have a lot of trash and debris in your yard, or if you live in a wooded area where there tends to be voluminous winter yard debris, consider renting a large trash container or dumpster and splitting the cost between neighbors. Most municipal waste management services can provide this service. For a couple hundred dollars you can rent a container for a day or two that will hold up to *20 cubic yards* of trash and debris (that's a *lot* of trash!). The temporary nature of the container makes it a great incentive to find every scrap of trash and debris in your house and yard and toss it in.

DESIGNATE A TIME TO CLEAN

Spring cleaning is much more likely to occur if you set aside a certain time for it and commit to it. Pick a weekend and make a list. Decide what jobs you want to accomplish, then prioritize the list.

Summer Solutions

Yard work becomes much more intensive during the summer months. Grass needs to be cut weekly, and weeds grow all season long. The trick to keeping yard work manageable is to do a little bit often, rather than letting it build up. Mow the grass one day, edge one day, weed one day, you get the idea. And, if you just can't stand the thought of all that time spent slaving away in the great outdoors, remember the teenager I urged you to hire earlier in the chapter. It's not too late to give him or her a call.

Summer is an ideal time to tackle other outdoor jobs, too, such as painting and roof repair. Chipped, flaking, peeling paint does more than just make the neighbors talk about the sad state of disrepair into which your house has fallen: it also lets damaging water and sunlight come into direct contact with wood, which can lead to wood rot. If you are considering either painting the outside of your house yourself or having it done by a professional, keep in mind that adequate preparation and high-quality paint or stain are the keys to a good, lasting paint job. Also, consider long-term wear when choosing paint colors. Saturated colors such as red and blue don't wear well and tend to fade in the sun, while more earthy tones such as beige, tan, and taupe look better, longer.

YOUR NEW BEST FRIEND, THE PRESSURE WASHER

Few products, gadgets, or appliances can make as much difference to the appearance of the outside of your home as a well-utilized power washer. With a few zippy strokes of the water wand of this labor-saving, environmentally friendly device, the accumulation of dirt, dust, mold, and debris from several months or even years literally washes away. A pressure washer can save you hours of scrubbing, scraping, and sweeping. Pressure washers are particularly useful for cleaning walkways and sidewalks, driveways, decks, and brick or stone patios.

Because a sturdy model can cost several hundred dollars, this is a good item to rent or pitch in and buy with friends or neighbors. Look for a power washer with a water pressure of at least 2,500 PSI (pounds per square inch).

When using a pressure washer, wear ratty old clothes and ear plugs. It's a noisy, messy job, but once you see the difference between the areas you have pressure-washed and the old, grimy areas that haven't yet been cleaned, you'll be hooked.

Great things to clean with a pressure washer:

✦ Sidewalks

✦ Walkways and stone paths

✦ Driveways

✦ Planters

✦ Vinyl siding

✦ Wood decks

✦ Stone edging and masonry

But, *don't* use a pressure washer on these things:

✦ Cars

✦ Gravel paths or walkways

✦ Roofs (unless you want a leaky roof, this is a job best left to the pros)

✦ Plants, pets, or children

✦ Anything painted (unless you *want* to remove degraded paint, in preparation for adding a new coat of paint or stain)

What You Need to Know about Swimming Pools

If you have a swimming pool in your backyard, then you already know how much work it takes to keep a pool sparkling. Many people spend a lot more time cleaning their pool than they actually spend swimming in it or enjoying its aesthetic appeal. If you are thinking about having a pool installed, first consider the substantial amount of time, effort, and resources that will be required to keep it looking good. After all, an ill-kept swimming pool is hardly an asset.

Most in-ground pools come with standard equipment: a pump and motor, skimmer baskets, and a filter. The motor drives the pump, which keeps the water circulating. Skimmer baskets remove large debris, such as leaves and small children's toys, and the filter removes fine particles from the water.

Chemicals are another vital component of swimming pools. Without adequate chlorination, your pool will rapidly degenerate into a dark and menacing cesspool.

Keeping pool water sanitized requires the regular addition of chemicals such as chlorine and bromine. The chemical levels must be carefully balanced: the water's alkalinity, pH level, water hardness, and total dissolved solids need to fall within certain ranges. Imbalanced water will result in cloudy water and potential eye irritation. Pool water needs to be tested about five times per week, and more often during periods of heavy pool use, substantial rainfall, or exceptionally hot weather.

HOW TO CLEAN A POOL

There are six basic steps involved in keeping a pool clean and sparkling:

- ✦ Adequate chemical balancing
- ✦ Regular cleaning of skimmer baskets and pool filter
- ✦ Skimming (the manual removal of surface debris)
- ✦ Vacuuming (to remove debris from the pool floor)
- ✦ Brushing (to remove algae buildup on the sides and bottom of the pool)
- ✦ Backwashing (the reversal of the pool's circulation system, which helps keep the filters clean and keeps the water flowing freely)

SEASONAL MAINTENANCE

In addition to regular pool maintenance, most pools need seasonal maintenance, as well (unless you live in a tropical region and your pool is used year-round).

Fitting your pool with a cover during the fall and winter months does a great job of keeping leaves and winter yard debris out of the water. If you use a pool cover, your work at the beginning of the season involves removing, cleaning, and storing the pool cover, as well as removing antifreeze chemicals from the plumbing system, starting the motor and pump, adding the first dose of chemicals, and refilling the water to the correct level.

Closing a pool for winter requires clearing water out of plumbing lines, adding antifreeze to the plumbing system, and covering the pool to help keep out winter debris.

PRACTICAL POOL TIPS

✦   Keep a rubber pan or small wading pool filled with water near the pool entrance so swimmers can rinse dirt, sand, and dust off their feet before stepping into the pool.

✦   If small critters tend to fall into the pool and drown overnight, rest a board on the edge of the pool with one end in the water, so that the waterlogged creatures can crawl out and escape.

✦   Keep a clothesline in an out-of-sight, sunny location for drying towels and swimsuits.

✦   Drill a few holes into the bottom of a large, plastic, lidded trash can and use it to store children's pool toys and floats.

✦   Only plant tidy evergreens near the perimeter of the pool. Plants that tend to shed a lot of needles, leaves, or blooms (such as pine trees or crepe myrtle) should be relegated to the front yard or removed altogether.

✦   An automatic pool sweep kicks up dirt and debris and keeps the bottom and sides of the pool relatively maintenance free.

✦ If pool maintenance is a constant aggravation, hire a professional pool maintenance company to keep it looking good.

Sand Solutions

For those who have a beach house, who visit the beach, or who have a sandbox in the backyard, here's a tip that will keep sand out of your house and car for good. Keep a stiff utility brush near all the places where sand threatens to encroach: in the trunk of the car, and/or by the back door. Use the implement to brush sand off feet, shoes, and from between toes *before* the sand gets tracked inside. You can also use the brush to beat sand out of beach towels before they are brought inside to wash.

Keep a small rubber pan of water near the back door (or whichever door tends to be used the most by sandy feet). Have children and sandy-toed adults step into the footbath before coming inside. (Hang a hand towel nearby so freshly washed feet can then be *dried* before entering.)

If you are truly plagued by sand dunes in your carpets, replace carpet with tile, stone, or vinyl flooring. If you go the tile route, make sure the tile is slightly textured, so it won't be overly slippery when wet. Slightly convex tiles laid with sand-colored grout are a great way to minimize the appearance of sand.

Finally, make sure exterior doors and windows are well sealed. Low-lying shrubs planted around the exterior of your home can also act as a filter for blowing sand.

Designate one entrance to be used for children coming in from playing outside. Use an outdoor clothesline where wet towels and swimsuits can be hung to dry. Install hooks for the easy storage of items such as swim fins and goggles.

Easy Outdoor Furniture Maintenance

The single best way to keep outdoor furniture looking like new is to keep it covered or otherwise protected during the weeks and months when it is not in use. You can buy a drawstring tarp at Home Depot for about $10 that easily covers most outdoor dining sets, chairs, or lounges, and it does a great job of protecting outdoor furniture from the elements.

Another tip: even though most outdoor chair pads claim to be weatherproof, or at least weather *resistant*, the truth is that these cushions won't last through more than a season or two if they are left to rot in the sun, wind, and rain. Bring them indoors or put them in the garage when they're not in use. (The Container Store sells a great outdoor cushion storage bag for $9.99.)

When spring arrives and it's time to get the outdoor furniture in tip-top shape, pay another visit to Home Depot, where you'll find spray bottles of cleansers such as SunBrite that are specially formulated to clean outdoor furniture. These cleansers not only clean vinyl, resin, aluminum, fiberglass, and wrought iron; they also add a tough, protective finish that helps the furniture withstand the onslaught of the elements. Once the furniture is clean, you can apply a thin coat of paste wax to most vinyl or metal surfaces, which will ease cleanup in the future.

Finally, if you are in the market for new outdoor furniture, do yourself a favor and avoid clear glass tabletops like the plague. They are an unequivocal nightmare to keep clean. Opt for tempered, textured glass or a cast iron or stone surface instead.

Get Those Windows Clean

Real estate agents often tell prospective home sellers to put away personal photos and mementos, get rid of clutter, and *clean their windows*. Why? Dull, dirty windows detract from the appearance of the whole house from both inside and out, while sparkling clean windows add an unmistakable polish. Clean windows improve the appearance of the whole house.

But windows are notoriously difficult to clean. To begin with, there are so many of them, and in many cases some if not all are difficult to reach; the job is intrinsically daunting.

Here are a few tips to make your glass and windows shine:

- ✦ Hire it done, but that doesn't mean you have to hire an expensive professional. If you get the right equipment, and show them how to do the quality job you want, you can hire a teenager from the neighborhood to do it at a fraction of the cost.

- ✦ Visit a janitorial supply store, where you can buy a professional sudser (a foam-covered wand that covers the entire window surface with just a few strokes) and squeegee. Professional window-washing equipment is often on telescoping wands that can reach even second-story windows with relative ease.

- ✦ To clean outdoor windows yourself, work the cleaner into a good lather in a bucket, apply it with the sudser, then let the cleaner sit for a minute or two. Then, using the squeegee, start at the top left-hand corner and draw the squeegee across the top and down the right-hand side of the glass. Repeat this motion, overlapping strokes until you reach the bottom of the pane. Keep an old towel handy to wipe the squeegee dry between strokes.

- ✦ For smaller window-cleaning jobs, use plain white paper towels and a glass cleaner. Spray the glass from a distance so the cleaner evenly distributes, then wipe from side to side inside and from top to bottom outside. If you see streaks when you're finished you'll be able to tell if they are on the inside or outside, based on the direction of the streaks.

- ✦ Remove, wash, and store window screens during the chilly fall and winter months. This protects them from the elements, plus you'll have a clear view for at least part of the year. In the spring, the windows will be easier to clean; then you can put the screens back in place in time for a new season of bugs and breezes.

TIP: A Tip from the Pros

When my friend Kathryn asked the professional window washers what they used to make the windows on her house so sparkly clean, she got a surprising answer: a few drops of liquid dishwashing soap and a splash of ammonia added to a bucket of hot water. Soap the windows, squeegee clean, then polish with a soft, clean rag. "My windows have never looked so good," says Kathryn, "and all they used was water, dish soap, and ammonia. Who knew?"

Never Clean Windows Again

Innovations in glass manufacturing are revolutionizing the way consumers clean windows—or don't clean them, as the case may be. A company called PPG has patented a technology called SunClean, which is a self-cleaning type of glass. How does it work?

During the manufacturing process, a durable, transparent coating is applied to hot glass, where it becomes an integral part of the glass surface. Photocatalytic properties in the glass help loosen and break down organic dirt and compounds, while hydrophilic properties in the glass cause water to sheet evenly over the glass instead of beading. The sheeting action helps flush the surface clean and speed drying, which discourages streaking and spotting. Put away the glass cleaner and the squeegee; the best way to make SunClean windows sparkle is to hose them down. For more information, visit www.ppgSunClean.com.

Deck Maintenance Tips

Home and garden magazines are filled with photos of gorgeous, pristine, immaculate decks. Like most home features portrayed in the magazines, however, the reality is that keeping a deck looking good doesn't just happen on its own. Many experts maintain that outdoor decks require every bit as much work and attention as indoor floors. Oh, great.

How, then, to outwit your deck?

Preventive maintenance is the key. Most deck damage is caused by stains, excessive moisture, or insect damage.

Stains on your deck can be minimized in two ways. First, be sure your deck is treated with a durable deck stain that can help repel grease, grime from foot traffic, and damage from excessive heat or moisture.

Next, determine the likely culprits that may cause deck damage and cut them off at the pass. One of the most damaging stains on decks is caused by excess grease that drips or spills from the runoff container beneath barbecue pits. Drain the container frequently. If you use the barbecue frequently, place a glass or Pyrex container beneath the grease trap, in case you forget to empty the container and you have an overflow. And when the deck does get dirty, hose it off with a pressure washer.

If your deck surface is close to the ground and air circulation is limited, cover the soil beneath the deck with a polyethylene barrier covered with decorative garden rock, to minimize damage caused by moisture trapped beneath the deck.

Finally, at the first sign of insect damage, drop everything and call an exterminator. Insects tend to view wood decks as one giant deadwood feast; if you ignore them, the damage to your deck will be swift and severe.

Autumn Checklist

With the arrival of fall you can count on two things: your yard won't need as much TLC as it did during the summer months, and the type of care it needs will be different.

Depending on where you live, fall may be a time to batten down the hatches, cover plants that are susceptible to cold, pull out fading annuals, and mulch heavily, to protect trees and shrubs from the oncoming freeze. This is also a good time to transplant or divide spring-blooming perennials.

In many areas fall is the best time to plant. Grass, trees, and shrubs all do better once the heat of summer has passed. They have the chance to build good, deep root systems—as opposed to merely hanging on for dear life during the heat of summer—but they need to get established before harsh winter conditions set in.

Once again, pay a visit to your local nursery or landscape gardener, who will happily tell you about your yard's specific seasonal needs.

Once the plants, trees, and shrubs are taken care of, turn your attention to other aspects of your house and yard:

✦ Cover outdoor furniture or put it in the garage, so it will be protected from excessive cold and moisture.

✦ Store outdoor décor items such as candles or small garden statues in the garage as well.

✦ Drain and winterize all outdoor faucets, and, if you have a sprinkler system, have a professional drain the lines before the first freeze.

Chapter Twelve

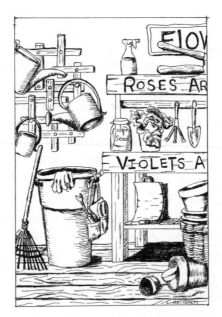

GARAGE, BASEMENT, ATTIC, SHED

Have you ever visited a well-kept home and had a chance to glance into the garage, basement, garden or tool shed, or attic, only to be astounded by the degree to which chaos appears to reign? If keeping a house neat and orderly can be a challenge, then keeping these spaces neat and orderly can be well-nigh impossible.

There are several reasons behind the apparent difficulty that many of us have in keeping these not-quite-inside/not-quite-outside rooms clean. First, they are not a part of the house that is typically the domain of one person. The whole family has to share these spaces. Here is the place for garden tools, the lawn mower, bags of mulch and grass seed, empty flower pots, trash and recycling bins, golf clubs, tennis racquets, infant strollers, muddy shoes that need to be cleaned, out-of-season clothes, holiday decorations, tools, and a whole host of other various, unrelated items.

Because these spaces are shared by all, it becomes difficult to develop a sense of ownership. What's the point in cleaning a space that everyone else will just trash again when you're finished? (This is a not-too-subtle variation of the sage observation that no one in the history of the world has ever washed a rental car.) So the garage or basement becomes the neglected stepchild of the house, the room that guests are never supposed to see, the place where Items Without a Home can be stashed with reckless abandon.

Another reason behind the difficulty in keeping these spaces clean is the relative filth of the items that tend to be stored in them. Dirty tools and garden equipment, remnant sawdust and wood shavings, muddy shoes, dripping wet and dirty vehicles, and maybe even kitty's litter box all share the space. A person could be forgiven for making the assumption that keeping the garage or basement clean is really, truly impossible.

But it's not.

There are three steps involved in outwitting these spaces:

1. Unused, worn-out, or remnant items need to be thrown away.

2. Everything else needs a designated storage space.

3. Everyone needs to pitch in once a month or so to straighten things up.

That's it. Let's look at each task separately.

If You're Not Using It, Throw It Away

In many cases a surplus of various items crammed into your garage or basement is not a result of inadequate storage space. Rather, in many if not most cases a garage or basement full of junk is a blinking neon sign that the occupants are plagued by *indecision*.

Do any of these internal discussions ring a bell?

Should I keep these old soccer trophies or throw them away? Maybe I'll wish I had them one day. Better hang on to them, just in case.

Hmm, these boxes are filled with old plates that are cracked and chipped. But maybe one of the kids will want them one day, anyway. Better hang on to them, just in case.

Now that I have a new set of golf clubs I can get rid of these old ones. Oh, wait. I might want to use them one day. They could be refurbished, and they'd be good as new. Better hang on to them, just in case.

Mental habits such as these are the reason many of us have a crowded, cluttered garage or basement. (I know one couple who has a four-car garage with so much stuff in it that they can't fit even *one* car into the garage. They know that no one *needs* that much *stuff*, yet they are wracked by indecision when it comes to throwing things away.)

Visualizing a tidy, clean space can help overcome these types of mental obstacles. With just a small amount of soul-searching, once you've had it with the mess and excess you will be able to connect the dots and see how your behavior is contributing to the problem.

Once I had really, truly had it with having a messy garage, I quit putting things there that had no place else to go. I found another place to put them, or I got rid of them altogether.

GETTING A GRIP ON HOLIDAY DÉCOR

Many of us have a tendency to collect lots of certain types of objects. I tend to hang on to holiday decorations, for example, long after the items serve any useful purpose whatsoever. One year I had eight large boxes of Christmas decorations. We decorated the house and I had five boxes left over, filled to the brim with tangled lights that didn't work, garish tinsel I no longer used, candles that had melted in storage, and wobbly Santas and reindeer with broken antlers. My husband looked at me, eyebrow raised. Why was I cluttering the garage with this useless junk?

I wasn't sure. Some of it had sentimental value. Some of it had resuscitation potential (I had plans to hot-glue candy canes around the melted candles, and they'd be good as new!). And some of it made it back into the boxes out of sheer laziness. In previous years I had tossed things back into the box in order to avoid dealing with them and making a decision.

I decided to cull through the boxes. I threw away decorations that hadn't been used for years. I hung on to a few items just for their sentimental value. And I whittled my collection down from eight boxes to three.

The next year, when it was time to decorate for the holidays, we pulled out the three boxes, and I was amazed. I didn't miss the things I'd thrown away a bit. Instead of having to pick through eight boxes filled with mostly useless rubbish, now I had three boxes of good, usable stuff.

Once the holidays were over, the next step was to carefully pack up the three boxes, but this time I labeled the boxes carefully. Now I have a manageable collection of decorations and I know where things are. And I have a lot more space in my garage. Everyone's happy.

Everything Needs a Place

The next step in ridding your garage, basement, or attic of junk and making it a pleasant, uncluttered part of your house: giving everything its very own place.

There are web sites, catalogs, and stores that sell lots of equipment and storage solutions. Bins, barrels, and racks can all be used to organize this space.

If you or someone in the house has a lot of tools and building supplies to keep stored and organized, then you may want to look into premade storage cabinets and shelving, which can keep tools and supplies clean, organized, and out of sight.

One of the best tips for storing tools that are used regularly is to use a round, canvas tool organizer. This miracle storage device slips into a five-gallon bucket and keeps tools organized, upright, and visible—no more rooting around in a dank, stinky toolbox for a screwdriver, flashlight, or chisel.

Screw a peg board to the wall to hang tools, saws, saw blades, and garden utensils. Hooks can be added and things can be rearranged on an as-needed basis, and you'll be able to quickly find what you're looking for since everything is stored in plain sight.

One time-honored way to keep small items such as nails, tacks, and screws organized is to use empty, clear baby food jars. If you have unused space beneath a shelf, nail the jar lids to the bottom edge of a shelf so the jars can be screwed into place. Or, invest in a compartmented toolbox outfitted with dividers that separate different types and sizes of hardware and fastenings. You'll never hunt for a nail or screw again.

Shelves mounted along the walls can dramatically improve the storage capacity in your garage or basement by utilizing previously wasted or cluttered space. For bulky items such as bicycles, use heavy-duty wall or ceiling hooks to get the objects off the floor and out of the way.

As you contemplate adding shelves, hooks, and bins, try to think three-dimensionally. Look up. Like closets, most garages have space near the ceiling that can be used to store seasonal or rarely used items. Mount shelves around the wall perimeter a few feet from the ceiling. Shelving can even be mounted *on the ceiling*, to take advantage of all available space. These shelves screw into ceiling studs then suspend storage racks 18 to 26 inches from the ceiling. Amazingly, these types of storage shelves can hold up to 250 pounds ($79.95–$99.95, 800-345-5789, www.GriotsGarage.com).

Ironically, lots of garages, basements, and sheds are cluttered by a disorganized, falling-down pile of cleaning tools and supplies. Wall-mounted hooks can provide a place for brooms and mops, and—an added bonus—the hooks help damp mops air-dry. Hang mops and cleaning supplies near a door or along a wall where circulating air and sunlight can help keep them from getting stale and musty. Another option: store brooms and mops, handles down, in a clean, empty trash can in a corner.

NEAT IDEAS FOR THE GARAGE

- ✦ A wire shoe rack near the door can provide a place for muddy or dirty shoes and boots.

- ✦ A memo board or cork board mounted on the outside of the door leading into the house is a great place to leave messages for those who come into the house through the garage.

- ✦ Don't hang on to old boxes or packing material; they're a favorite hiding place for roaches and silverfish.

- ✦ Got mice in the garage? Got a cat in the house? Crack the garage door an inch, then have kitty sleep in the garage for a few nights. Problem solved. Alternative solutions include keeping the cat litter box in the garage, or, if you don't have a cat, placing a few small containers of used kitty litter near garage entrances. (You can get some from a pet store or local vet.)

- ✦ Rinse cans and bottles before you throw them away to avoid stinky garbage smells in the garage.

Keeping It Clean

Once clutter has been dealt with and the items in your garage, basement, and other storage areas are neatly organized, the next task is to keep it all clean.

If you live with others, cleaning the garage or basement shouldn't be a job for one person. Once a month, have a Garage (or Basement) Cleaning Fest. Everyone rolls up their sleeves and pitches in to put things where they belong, straighten shelves, clear off flat surfaces, and throw away trash. Then order pizza when you're done.

There are a few tools and tricks that can help make cleaning these spaces quick and easy:

A ShopVac—an outdoor vacuum cleaner—can quickly take care of dust, cobwebs, and sawdust. Prices start at about $60. Or you can use a garden blower to blow dust and leaves right back outside, where they belong (be sure to wear goggles).

Sprinkle non-clumping kitty litter or sawdust on grease stains on the garage floor, then vacuum or sweep it up the next day.

A duster mounted on a telescoping pole can swish away cobwebs in hard-to-reach corners and crevices.

Finally, make sure the light in your garage or basement is good. Replace burned-out light bulbs or install long-lasting fluorescent tubes. Like the rest of the house, these spaces are much easier to keep clean when you can see what you're doing.

TIP: *The Beauty of Utility Sinks*

Consider installing a utility sink in the garage, basement, garden shed, or laundry room. You will be amazed at all the ways a utility sink will come in handy. Dirty shoes, paintbrushes, garden tools, and more can be easily cleaned without dragging stuff inside and dirtying up the kitchen sink.

---

7 Home Repairs You Can't Ignore

✦ A water leak…anywhere. Left unchecked, a water leak can lead to rot, dry rot, mold, and termite infestation. Take steps to remedy leaks as soon as you notice a problem.

✦ Faulty wiring. If you notice flickering lights, you may have too
  many appliances hooked to one circuit, or faulty wiring. Either
  one can lead to a fire. Consult an electrician to help determine
  and then correct the problem.

✦ Rodent infestations. Rats, mice, and squirrels do more than
  chew through priceless family heirlooms stored in the basement
  or attic: they also love to chew through insulation and wiring.
  These critters are the cause of many house fires. Call a professional exterminator at the first sign of scurrying little visitors.

✦ Faltering furnace. If you notice a sudden spike in your gas or oil
  bill, the culprit could be a faulty furnace, which can cause
  deadly carbon-monoxide buildup in your home. Have your furnace professionally cleaned and inspected annually.

✦ A smoking chimney. Chimneys that aren't properly cleaned and
  maintained can catch fire due to creosote buildup. Having the
  chimney cleaned annually costs about $100.

✦ Dirty (or missing) air-conditioning filters. Filthy or missing filters allow dirt and dust to settle on air-conditioning coils. Warm
  air passing over the coils causes condensation, which results in a
  muddy coating that is the perfect medium for growing mold
  and bacteria, which then gets blown all over the house. Enough
  mud can keep air from getting into the system and can start a
  fire. Many air-conditioning failures can be traced to this simple
  lack of maintenance.

✦ Blocked dryer vents. The humble clothes dryer causes more than
  15,000 fires every year, which are often caused by a buildup of lint
  in the duct that vents to the outside. Clean the ducts regularly.

Chapter Thirteen

ENTERTAINING WITH EASE

For those who find keeping their house straight and clutter-free to be anything less than second nature, the thought of entertaining guests can induce an apoplectic fit. "How can I have guests," you may wonder, "when I can barely keep my head above water when it comes to keeping this house clean?"

The question to ask yourself is not whether you can afford the time and energy to entertain your family and friends. The question is whether you can afford *not* to. Before we get into the nitty-gritty of entertaining with ease, it's important to remember the purpose of spending time with friends and family in the first place. Keep your eye on the goal of reinforcing these vital relationships.

If housekeeping is not your strongest suit, chances are good that your close friends and family members know this about you already (and love you anyway). The goal is not to impress, to show off your silverware or shiny floor, or even to showcase your formidable culinary talents. Rather, the goal is to spend enjoyable, quality time with those you hold dear.

So, relax. Keep it easy. You don't have to pull out all the stops to spend time with those you care about. You don't have to have someone over to your house every weekend. You can meet at a restaurant, invite a friend to join you for a movie or to see a play, or you can meet at the park and have a picnic together.

There are times, however, when you will probably want to have friends join you in your home, and the fact is that there is something uniquely bonding about spending time with someone in their element. It's warm and generous and intimate. Having friends over for dinner is a delightful social gesture.

If your home isn't yet to the point where you feel free inviting others to visit, don't worry. Use the methods and strategies in this book, and you'll get there. In fact, you may even want to use the prospect of inviting friends over as a goal to set for yourself once you have control of your house and everything in it.

QUICK 5: KEYS TO EASY ENTERTAINING

1. Rely on prepared foods to minimize your time in the kitchen.
2. Have everyone bring a dish.
3. As you prepare, clean as you go.
4. Have everyone in the family pitch in to help get things ready.
5. Don't worry about having a spotless house. Dim the lights and forget about it.

Plan Ahead

First on the agenda: get organized. Making plans well in advance of having a party or entertaining guests is critical if you want to make the time enjoyable for everyone.

Have you ever been to the grocery store the day before Thanksgiving? The chaos is pure and unmitigated. The truly vexed shoppers on this date are those who have no list, who are wandering in a daze from aisle to aisle, clearly unprepared for the events that lie ahead.

If you had been in that same store a day or two before, you would have seen an entirely different bunch. The shoppers then were serene, happy even, shopping from carefully prepared lists with the confidence that only comes from adequate preparation.

The importance of planning ahead to facilitate easy entertaining doesn't apply only to major holidays. When you have visiting guests from out of town or even friends over for dinner, the admonition to be prepared still holds true. The more work you do in advance, the less you'll have to do once your guests arrive.

The key to ensuring a successful event of any stripe is a relaxed host and/or hostess. It doesn't matter if the house is decorated like a department-store window and the food is worthy of *Bon Appétit*: if the hosts aren't having a good time, no one else will have a good time, either. It's no fun to be a guest who is stressing out the hosts by merely being present. So plan ahead, get the food and drinks ready in advance, spiff up the house a bit, and then *relax* and enjoy the opportunity to spend time with friends.

Different Types of Entertaining

Let's look at a few different possible events you can host. We'll break it down by how easy a particular event is to host, from a simple evening of guests for dinner, to having visitors for several days, all the way to hosting an elaborate holiday celebration for extended family and friends.

Before anyone comes to your home as an invited guest, there are four areas to consider:

1. Getting the house clean

2. What drinks to offer

3. What food to serve

4. What entertainment to provide

Now, let's look at each of these events and all that they entail separately:

HAVING FRIENDS FOR DINNER

Level of Difficulty: 1

If you want to expand your social life and reinforce your relationships, inviting friends to dinner is a great way to do it. Dinner can be simple or elaborate, but the one factor that remains a constant is that inviting friends for dinner is an unmistakable social sign of warmth and friendliness.

The late Erma Bombeck once wrote that if she had her life to live over again, she would invite friends over for dinner more and worry about a faded sofa or stains on the rug less. What a wise woman.

So, you want to have friends for dinner. The place to start is to set a date and invite them. Give them at least a week's notice, and, when you discuss the date and time, ask them if they have any strong food preferences, likes or dislikes, or if they are allergic to anything such as peanuts or seafood.

Next, plan to have the house looking good, although most guests who come for dinner don't expect perfection. Straighten centrally located rooms, freshen the powder room, dust, vacuum, then don't worry about the rest. This is a simple dinner with friends, not a State Dinner with the Queen of England.

If you run short on time to spiff up the house, do as my mother-in-law Mildred suggests and make sure you dust the floorboards in the powder room. Why? "This is the one spot that guests always notice," says Mildred. "Even if the rest of the house isn't spotless, I always make sure that I pay attention to that one small detail!"

Plan the menu a few days in advance. This is not the time to try anything new or fancy. For entertaining ease, opt for simple, classic dishes every time.

Entertaining guru Ina Garten, author of *Barefoot Contessa Parties!*, offers this sage advice for having guests in your home: Plan on serving food that has been prepared in advance. In her words, "I can't say enough about *assembling* food rather than *cooking*." If you can't decide between serving roasted chicken with dilled new potatoes or fresh seafood crêpes that you make once the guests arrive, opt for the chicken every time.

Have drinks ready to serve, and make sure you have plenty of ice on hand before your guests arrive. I like to set up a portion of the kitchen counter with all the drink supplies set out so guests can serve themselves once things get rolling.

For small, intimate dinners you may not need to plan much, if anything, in the way of entertainment, but do make sure that the setting is charming and a bit out of the ordinary. In the winter, have a fire roaring in the fireplace; in warmer weather set an outdoor table with fresh flowers and lots of candles. Keep in mind that you are *entertaining* your guests for the evening. This is like recess for adults. Have something fun to do.

What's fun? Look at the details of the evening. Is a pot roast fun? Not really. Are steamed clams dipped in drawn butter fun? Definitely. Wine is okay, but margaritas are *fun*. Artichoke dip? Ho hum. Pot stickers on confetti rice? Better. A fancy Saturday night sit-down dinner with linen napkins and bone china can be Dullsville, but a clambake on the beach? Fun fun fun.

In many instances it is actually easier to host a novel, innovative gathering than the traditional sit-down meal. For example, it's easier to have friends over to fondue or barbecue than it is to host a six-course dinner. So, plan something fun and simple—and a little bit out of the ordinary—and your evening with friends will be enjoyable for all.

HAVING VISITORS FOR SEVERAL DAYS

Level of Difficulty: 2

When house guests are expected, planning ahead becomes even more important. It's an uncomfortable feeling to visit someone if they haven't prepared for your visit in advance: meals, accommodations, and entertainment should all at least be sketched out before your guests arrive. It's easy to change plans, but difficult to be a gracious host without some sort of a blueprint to go by.

If guests are expected to stay for more than a day or two, you'll want to include them in meal preparation. Plan on serving simple hors d'oeuvres with beverages in the evenings as you cook, and give your guests a simple job to do, like setting the table, so they won't feel as though they aren't contributing.

For visits that last more than a few days, build some free time into your schedule for both you and your guests; it will give you all a break from constant visiting and can provide what may be a much-needed breather for everyone.

So, how to simplify the task of hosting guests in your home? Here are a few pointers:

✦ Avoid using your guest room, if you have one, as a junk room. If you have piled a bunch of IWAH (Items Without a Home) into this room, then preparing to have the room actually used by visiting guests can be a nightmare. Avoid this unpleasant scenario by keeping the room at least moderately straight and neat even when guests aren't expected for some time.

✦ If you do use the room for something besides visitors, keep the activity contained. (One woman who uses her guest room for scrapbooking keeps all her supplies in a bookshelf in the room.

When she expects guests she simply cleans up the scrapbooking table in the corner, and she's done.)

✦ Plan on easy-to-assemble meals that don't require a lot of intensive kitchen work. Have meat or vegetables marinating in a zip-lock bag, for example, and ready to throw on the grill. Many upscale grocery stores carry delicious, ready-to-cook meals that can be quickly and easily prepared. You want to avoid anything elaborate; opt for the simple every time.

✦ Make the room in which your guests will be sleeping as private and comfortable as possible. Everyone will be more at ease if your guests have a comfortable retreat where they can retire or seek a bit of solitude now and then.

✦ Plan activities to get everyone out of the house. Take your guests on a long walk, or head out on a day trip to see local area attractions.

✦ Keep up with basic cleaning and maintenance even though you have guests. If you let things go to pot, soon the whole house will be trashed and no one will be comfortable.

HOSTING A HOLIDAY BASH

Level of Difficulty: 3

Even for those who manage to keep their home relatively clean and uncluttered for most of the year, nothing inspires fear like looming holidays.

Seasoned veteran hosts know the drill: you spend days and even weeks cooking, baking, and cleaning your house meticulously, only to have the whole shebang go up in smoke in a matter of hours. Visiting guests arrive laden with packages and hearty appetites, pleasantries are exchanged, crumbs are dropped and drinks are sloshed as shredded wrapping paper begins to mount, then, before you know it, the party's over and the guests begin filtering out, leaving you to deal with the mess.

For those who have been repeatedly burned by this discouraging scenario, there are a few strategies you can use to reclaim the holidays and make them stress-free events.

The first and most important rule for hosting a successful, stress-free bash? Delegation.

It's that simple. If you want to maintain a modicum of sanity, you can't do it all yourself. Don't even try.

As with other types of entertaining, you do need to be organized, but this type of organization is different. You don't have to get it all figured out so you can *do it all yourself;* instead, you have to get it all figured out so you can *assign portions of it to others*.

Break it down by categories: food, drinks, setup, decorations. If you really want to make it easy, assign a cleanup crew, too.

What you are able to assign will depend on the number of guests you are inviting. For smaller gatherings, or those of 10 or fewer, you can keep things pretty simple. Have someone bring an appetizer, someone bring a dessert, and you can provide the rest. But for larger gatherings, don't be shy about asking for help—and asking for specifics. Don't say, "Oh, just bring yourself!" Say, "Oh, it would be great if you could bring along a bottle of wine" (or dessert, or appetizer, or whatever it is you need for them to bring).

Next, put early birds to work once they arrive. Parties are more fun when everyone pitches in and pulls it off together. Ask someone to light candles or show guests where to put their coats. Again, you could do it all by yourself, but the idea here is to spread the work out so that no one (not even you) is unfairly burdened. And remember, your guests won't be able to fully enjoy themselves if you are dashing about 100 mph with your hair on fire, as my mother vividly notes.

For very large gatherings, consider hiring someone to come in and help. You can hire anyone from a local teenager to a professional cook or cleaning service to come in and help with getting things ready, serving food or drinks once guests arrive, or cleaning up at the end of the event.

Family gatherings where lots of kids and presents are involved can get cluttered quick. Keep a box of trash bags on hand and have your family and guests put the trash into the bag as soon as they unwrap a gift. Or, if you'd rather, wait until everyone is finished unwrapping gifts, then have everyone pitch in and pick up the trash.

15 Tips for a Great Party Menu

1. Keep it simple. If it's an hors d'oeuvres and drinks affair, for example, then you'll want to serve finger foods that can be consumed easily, without having to use unwieldy utensils. Many upscale grocery stores and markets carry delicious frozen hors d'oeuvres that can be prepared and served in less than 15 minutes.

2. Plan a menu that allows you to make most, if not all, of the dishes ahead of time. Think through the work that will be required between courses, and minimize the amount of last-minute food preparation that will need to be done by either preparing in advance or eliminating fussy recipes altogether.

3. Think about how your oven and cooktop will need to be used. You want to avoid having six dishes that all need to be heated at the same time.

4. Avoid serving foods with overpowering aromas, such as certain types of fish, cabbage, or dishes with lots of garlic or bacon. The taste and smell will overpower the other dishes you are serving.

5. Plan ahead for how you will present the food. Set the table or buffet in advance with the serving dishes you are planning on using, and use Post-it notes to designate which foods will be served in which bowls or platters. There's nothing worse than pulling a roast out of the oven then not having a place to put it!

6. To minimize post-party cleanup, consider serving a variety of appetizers on a single serving platter, instead of giving each dish its own plate.

7. Serve simple, delicious dishes that you are familiar with and that you have prepared before. This is not the time to try something new!

8. Make one or two dishes the focus of the meal, then keep the rest of the menu items fairly simple and low-key. Too many splashy items is unnecessary overkill.

9. Remember to serve a variety of foods that can accommodate different dietary needs or restrictions. Plan on a serving a vegetarian dish and one or two low-fat selections, so that all your guests can find something they can eat.

10. Serve a big basket of bakery-style rolls, so guests who may still be hungry after the meal (heaven forbid!) can "fill in the holes" with bread.

11. Plan on having drinks ready to serve and hors d'oeuvres ready to go at least 15 minutes before you expect your guests to arrive.

12. Wear something simple and comfortable. The last thing you need to be worried about when you have guests is your appearance.

13. To keep things easy, serve an elegant, store-bought cake or dessert.

14. Use festive, disposable party-ware for informal events to minimize post-party cleanup.

15. Hire a cleanup crew to come put your house back in order the morning after the party.

Keeping Holiday Décor Simple

It took me many years of full-fledged decorating for the holidays to come to the realization that a few beautifully decorated focal points in the house are every bit as festive and enjoyable as having the entire house dripping with tinsel.

Whereas I once decked every hall, now I opt for two or three central spots and decorate just those areas with reckless abandon. The rest of the house pretty much stays serene and uncluttered.

Make sure the areas you choose to decorate are centrally located. Put the Christmas tree in the front window of the house, for example, or a Menorah in a place where it's sure to be seen and appreciated.

The mantel is another obvious, central location for holiday décor. A mantel cloak, stockings, candles, or garland can make this ordinary family room fixture sparkle with holiday cheer.

Many types of holiday decorations are messy and should be avoided if your goal is to minimize the amount of work you're going to need to do to keep things looking even sort of clean.

For example, as much as I love the scent of a real Christmas tree, the needles, water, and sap have collectively discouraged me from using the real thing. We now have a gorgeous *faux* tree with the lights already attached. It takes about half an hour to set up—less than the amount of time it takes to go out and buy a real tree—and I don't spend one minute picking up stray pine needles. (I do miss the scent of the real thing, however, so I buy a real fir wreath to put on the front door. It's elegant, simple, and the dropping pine needles stay *outside*, where they belong.)

Other decorations to avoid include anything flocked, anything that sprays out of a can, and anything that comes with 1,500 individual pieces or strands, such as popcorn garlands or tiny strips of tinsel. Just say no.

Opt instead for large, simple, but dramatic centerpieces. I have a large metal candle holder in the shape of a Christmas tree that holds about 30 votive candles. It's simple, elegant, gorgeous when lit, inexpensive to maintain, and easy to set up and store. I love it. It gives the whole room a festive glow when it's lit, but doesn't require any work or cleanup once the holidays are through. It just gets put back in the closet, where it waits until it can light up a table the following year.

Another simple idea for easy holiday décor: fill crystal bowls with shiny glass ornaments or balls. Once candles are lit around the bowls, the balls and ornaments give off a gorgeous sparkle. It's quick and easy, easily contained, and beautiful to behold.

Keep in mind that during the holidays, lots of the festive decorations arrive with and in anticipation of having guests. Holiday serving

platters are brought out; brightly wrapped presents arrive. Lavish dis-
plays of delectable hors d'oeuvres, pastries, and presents match the glitter of store-bought decorations any day.

TIP: *Never Fight Tangled Holiday Lights Again*

The Container Store has an ingenious product that keeps
holidays cords neatly wrapped. For a mere $1.99, this
plastic frame allows you to wrap holiday lights neatly
instead of bunching them together and hoping for the best.

Happily, wreath storage boxes, ornament storage
containers, gift wrap organizers, and dinnerware storage
containers are also available at The Container Store.

TIP: *An Easy Way to Polish Silver*

Silver is beautiful but it can be a pain in the neck to polish
and keep clean. Here's an easy way to remove tarnish
quickly: Put a 5-inch square of aluminum foil in the bottom
of a large, non-aluminum pan. Add water: for every quart,
add 1 teaspoon salt and 1 teaspoon baking soda. Bring to a
boil. Drop in the silver you want to polish, leaving each
piece in for two to three minutes, or until the tarnish is
gone. (Note: Do not use this method if you like a little bit of
tarnish to remain, to enhance the patina or otherwise give
the silver character. This method removes it all.) Like magic,
the tarnish will transfer from the silver to the aluminum foil.
When you remove the silver, if any spots remain, polish
clean with a damp rag dipped in baking soda, then rinse
with warm water and dry with a soft cloth.

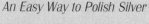

Adopt a Realistic Holiday Strategy

Managing expectations is key if you want to enjoy the holidays, but this is much easier to do in theory than in actual practice. Here are a few tips to help you keep your expectations somewhat realistic:

+ As you plan a party, keep in mind the various quirks and personalities of the people you are inviting. If you have a crazy uncle who drinks too much at parties, odds are good that he will not jump onto the wagon just for *your* party, so plan accordingly. Maybe limit the amount of alcohol you serve to only beer and wine, or make arrangements ahead of time for someone to drive him home if necessary, so you won't have to have a big *someone-steal-Uncle-Ned's-car-keys-before-he-gets-behind-the-wheel* brouhaha as the evening winds to a close.

+ Limit the number of gourmet magazines you read or cooking/ entertainment television shows you watch before hosting an event. Those shows are put on with the collective efforts of literally dozens of professionals. Don't try to compete with the pros unless you just happen to be a Domestic Goddess perfectionist yourself.

+ Delegate parts of the party preparations to others. Have everyone bring a dish. Everyone enjoys a potluck, where every guest has the opportunity to showcase a special dish but no one is stuck with having to cook for 20 (or 30…or more).

+ If the thought of hosting a large gathering makes you nervous, then downsize things a bit. Do you really need to invite the entire neighborhood to your Holiday Open House? Instead of inviting 30 people, invite 10. And if the thought of hosting a bash at your house just unnerves you completely, then arrange to meet friends at a centrally located restaurant instead.

✦ If you are looking forward to hosting a party for a few friends or family members you rarely get to see, then make arrangements to see them either a few days before the party or a few days after. This will take the pressure off of having to visit with everyone during such a short, busy window of time, and will alleviate any disappointment once your guests are gone that you "hardly got to spend any time with so-and-so."

Common Holiday Stains and How to Remove Them

Once the holidays are in full swing, you may find yourself dealing with one or more of these troublesome stains. Here are some easy ways to remove some of the worst offenders:

✦ **Grease stains.** Remember that grease removes grease. Rub a dab of Crisco into the stain, let sit for a few minutes to loosen the stain, and then launder as usual.

✦ **Chocolate.** If the item is not washable, take it to the dry cleaners. If it can be washed, treat the stain with warm, sudsy water, then blot. Next, add a mixture of one part ammonia and three parts warm water, then blot again. Or try a cleaning solvent such as Carbona (lay the garment on an absorbent towel and apply the solvent to the back of the stain). Blot, then launder as usual.

✦ **Cranberry** (or any fruit stain, for that matter). Use a rubber band to pull the fabric taut over a bowl. Cover the stain with salt, then set the bowl down in a deep kitchen or utility room sink. From a height of two or three feet, pour a kettle of boiling water over the stain.

✦ **Red wine.** Blot to remove every drop that you possibly can, then treat with white wine. Blot the white wine up, then apply a layer of salt. Let the salt dry, then vacuum. Club soda can be used instead of white wine.

✦ **Water rings on wood.** Carefully rub the stain with very-fine-gauge steel wool rubbed in paste wax.

Less Is More

In many cases the sheer volume of *stuff* after the holidays makes us feel weighty and bloated. Gifts we didn't want or need fill nooks and crannies we worked so hard during the year to clean off. In a world where so many suffer from hunger and a need for basic things like clothing and shelter, the excess of the holiday season can leave us feeling guilty and overwhelmed.

The solution to wretched excess is simple: talk to those with whom you regularly exchange gifts and tell them how you feel.

Some families have gotten into the habit of giving gifts in quantity over quality, but the reality is that in most cases one high-quality item is more valuable than 10 cheap knockoffs. I'd take one good pair of wool socks over a whole bag of cheap polyester any day.

So decide, together with those with whom you exchange gifts, to scale down your holiday gift-giving and make it more meaningful. One couple in Grapevine, Texas, decided that Christmas had gotten way too materialistic, so they decided to give each other only handmade gifts… that didn't cost more than ten dollars to make! What on earth can you do with only ten dollars? The husband carved a wooden paperweight in the shape of a cross to go on his wife's desk. She made shadow portraits of the kids with black construction paper and a couple of inexpensive frames, to hang in his office. The gifts were thoughtful and they required time and careful consideration. "That was our best Christmas ever," the wife exclaimed.

Here are a few ideas for ways you can change a bloated, excessive holiday pattern that only adds to household clutter and waste:

- ✦ Agree on a preset spending limit.

- ✦ For your immediate family, set a limit on how many gifts you'll buy for each person. Let the kids know of your plan in advance, so they won't be surprised by only a few high-quality presents if they've been accustomed to dozens of smaller gifts in the past.

- ✦ Decide on a theme for gifts each year, such as "Great Books" or "Pictures and Photos." This enables you to do most of your holiday shopping all at once, in only one or two stores, instead of running yourself ragged by shopping for twenty different items in twenty different stores.

- ✦ Pull names out of a hat so that you only have to buy a gift for one person.

- ✦ Agree to buy gifts only for the children.

- ✦ Ask people if there is anything they would like.

- ✦ Buy a gift certificate to their favorite store.

- ✦ Give a gift certificate to a wonderful restaurant, or for services such as a day at the spa.

- ✦ Plan on a holiday meal together in lieu of exchanging gifts.

- ✦ Agree to give only homemade gifts.

A Few Final Thoughts

Outwitting housework is about much more than having a clean, organized home. Outwitting housework is about control: controlling what comes into your home and how, and controlling the processes that work to keep things neat and orderly.

As you've seen, this is not a book about thousands of ways to clean anything and everything in your house, boat, or car. This is a book about understanding the areas where you tend to have trouble, understanding why, then making conscious decisions to alter the dynamics that keep your home in disarray.

As you set about the task of learning to outwit housework, keep in mind the value of making maintenance-free decisions. For example, if your house is dusty, then the solution is not to dust more frequently, but to find and then remove the primary sources of dust in your home. If you want to buy a house plant, don't buy a fern, which will begin shedding the minute it crosses the threshold into your home. Buy an ivy or pothos instead, which will need a bit of water every month or so and may drop a leaf once in a blue moon.

We've seen literally hundreds of ways to simplify the process of keeping your house, yard, and vehicle clean. Now the rest is up to you. *Actively* look for ways to simplify the processes you use to maintain the spaces in which you and your family live. What is at stake is much more than whether or not any visiting toddlers should be encouraged to eat off the floor. What is at stake is the comfort level you and your family experience in those valuable hours when you're at home, whether or not your home is a refuge or a source of frustration in your life.

Remember that the process of outwitting housework is a marathon, not a sprint. If you have developed poor housekeeping habits through the years, then odds are good that learning new ways of doing things will take time. Be patient, and be gentle with yourself and your family. Revamping your approach to such a crucial area of your life takes time and determination.

Finally, once you have reevaluated your approach, determined which areas need work, and found better, more efficient processes, tell me about it! I would love to hear about your successes in outwitting housework. Please visit my website at www.OutwittingStress.com, and send any comments or suggestions for future editions of *Outwitting Housework* to Nancy@OutwittingStress.com.

Chapter Fourteen

SOURCE GUIDE

Automobiles:
www.GriotsGarage.com

Babies:
www.DiaperNet.com

Cleaning tips:
www.FlyLady.net

Closets and storage:
www.ClosetMaid.com
www.EasyClosets.com
www.SmartFurniture.com

Consumer information:
www.ConsumerReports.com

General storage:
www.ContainerStore.com
www.HoldEverything.com
www.OrganizedHome.com
www.ShopGetOrganized.com

Pets:
www.BestFriendsCompany.net

Photo management services and software:
www.ArcSoft.com
www.ClubPhoto.com
www.Ofoto.com
www.PhotoMeister.com

Light Impressions
www.LightImpressionsDirect.com

Specialty products:
www.Caldrea.com
www.RustSolver.com
www.PlumbingStore.com
www.StarFibers.com

Sports equipment / storage:
www.WolverineSports.com

Stain removal:
www.CloroxLaundry.com
www.FabricLink.com
www.GoClean.com

Windows:
www.ppgSunClean.com

Index